Kidney Friendly Diet Cook Book:

Recipes for a Pre-Dialysis Kidney Disease Lifestyle

By Mathea Ford, RD/LD

WHAT THIS BOOK IS ABOUT

In this book chock full of recipes, you will find many ways to enjoy your meals. First, as a person on a pre-dialysis renal diet, you need to understand the diet you are on. Inside is plenty of great information that teaches you how and why you should limit certain foods and nutrients when following this plan.

Inside you will find recipes in many categories for all meals, from breakfast to dinner. There are 5 breakfast recipes, including an applesauce nut muffin recipe that I serve to my family on weekends and freeze individually to eat during the week. You also get 9 beef recipes – including a meatloaf recipe that meets your dietary needs. You have an equal number of pork recipes – 9 – with a couple of yummy pork chop recipes you'll serve over and over again. Next, there are 8 poultry recipes, with a delicious tarragon turkey recipe that I serve often to my family because they love the tartness of the sauce. Now, for seafood lovers, there are 10 recipes that will make your mouth water – especially the roasted shrimp and broccoli.

In an effort to not neglect those who do not eat meat, I have 6 recipes that are vegetarian, including my favorite, Pumpkin Pasta. And 6 salad recipes, which contain a variety of flavors from chicken to pork. Soups are very popular, and you get 9 soups, but most importantly – 3 broths that are easy to make and low sodium for you to use in any dish. I have 17 side dishes and 4 desserts to round out the book and make it easy for you to create a meal with the recipes in this book.

As a special gift for those interested in this topic, I have an email series that is 7 lessons and provides additional information about cooking for people with chronic kidney disease. I have some baking and conversions information for those just getting started cooking, as well as some equipment suggestions, plus tips and tricks for making delicious recipes and finding the best ingredients.

Go to this link: http://www.renaldiethq.com/e-course-kidney-friendly-diet-cookbook/

Now, onto the cookbook and more information!

TABLE OF CONTENTS

AN OVERVIEW OF KIDNEY DISEASE

(If you want indepth information about kidney disease and all the ways you can prevent it, please get my book entitled – *Living With Chronic Kidney Disease – PreDialysis* available on kindle and in paperback on amazon.com – links in the back of the book)

Kidney disease is a complex process that works on your body and organs and eventually causes your kidneys to stop working. It usually happens over a period of time. Approximately 23 Million US Adults have Chronic Kidney Disease. That is an average of 11% of the population, a little over one in 10 people.

Wikipedia defines kidney disease as:

"**Chronic kidney disease** (CKD), also known as **chronic renal disease**, is a progressive loss in renal function over a period of months or years. The symptoms of worsening kidney function are non-specific, and might include feeling generally unwell and experiencing a reduced appetite. Often, chronic kidney disease is diagnosed as a result of screening of people known to be at risk of kidney problems, such as those with high blood pressure or diabetes and those with a blood relative with chronic kidney disease. Chronic kidney disease may also be identified when it leads to one of its recognized complications, such as cardiovascular disease, anemia or pericarditis."

This book is for people who are in the stages of kidney disease PRIOR to dialysis. I see a lot of cookbooks for people on dialysis, and very few that cater to your needs prior to dialysis. Prior to dialysis, you have a need for low protein in your diet. You may or may not need potassium and phosphorus restriction.

eGFR – is known as the estimated glomerular filtration rate. Your kidneys have small blood vessels that act as filters known as glomerulus where the actual exchange between your blood and urine occurs. So the laboratory tries to calculate the rate that your kidneys are processing blood based on your creatinine levels, and adjusts it based on your age, sex and race through research tested formulas. When your eGFR is decreasing, it is a good indicator of your level of progression in kidney disease. As your eGFR rate decreases, patients become more lethargic, urine volume decreases and you may develop nausea or vomiting.

THE STAGES OF KIDNEY DISEASE ARE AS FOLLOWS:

Stage 1: Kidney damage with an eGFR ≥ 90 ml/min is considered stage 1 kidney disease. It is important to note that most people do not even realize they have kidney disease at this stage.

Stage 2: Kidney damage with an eGFR of 60-89 ml/min is considered stage 2 kidney disease. You have mild kidney disease, but note that if you have protein in your urine (trace, 1+ or 2+) you need to be assertive and discuss with your doctor how to slow down the process of moving to stage 3 kidney disease.

Stage 3: An eGFR of 30-59 ml/min is considered stage 3 kidney disease, with or without known damage. You have moderate to severe kidney disease, and you probably have protein in your urine. At this stage, you need to intervene with diet in order to significantly slow the progression of the disease.

Stage 4: When you have an eGFR of 15-29 ml/min it is considered stage 4 kidney disease. You can continue to make the important dietary and medical changes that your doctor recommends to reduce the rate of the progression to dialysis. You are on the doorstep of dialysis and should realize that you need to take drastic action if you have not done so up to now.

Stage 5: Stage 5 kidney disease is when your eGFR falls below 15 ml/min. You are at about 10% of your kidneys capacity still functional. You are likely to be preparing for dialysis at this time. It is not the end of the world if you are on dialysis, and as a matter of fact, many people who have been sick for so long can find dialysis makes them feel better because the waste product is being removed from their blood on a regular basis.

Next step is End Stage Renal Disease and Dialysis – your kidneys have reached the point of no return and you need dialysis to survive. You may be a candidate for transplant, but you will likely have to start dialysis until one becomes available. You might be working with a nephrologist in stages 4-5 to get access done and ready for dialysis.

OVERVIEW OF THE KIDNEY DIET AND RESTRICTIONS

Many people do not find out that they even have kidney disease until they are in stages 3 or 4, or a traumatic event and they may need to start dialysis abruptly. On my website, I hear the phrase, "what happened to stages 1 – 2?" Wherever you find yourself, I hope that you find some recipes you love in this book and a way to move forward controlling your diet and slowing the progression of kidney disease. It is unusual for people to go backwards and become stage 3 after moving to stage 4, but you can slow down the speed at which the damage to your kidneys continues to occur.

Part of the struggle of this diet is that you have to eat a very restrictive nutrient diet and try to get enough to eat but not too much of the nutrients that your body has difficulty processing. Here is an overview of the nutrients you need in your diet that are affected by kidney disease and influence the rate of progression of kidney failure.

1. Fluids can be significant in your diet. Most likely after you begin on dialysis, you will have a fluid restriction. But as your kidneys become more damaged and less effective, they fail to remove fluids properly. In your body, kidneys are responsible for removing wastes and extra fluids and turning it into urine. When your kidneys no longer make urine, you are going to need a fluid restriction. Fluid restrictions are not likely in stage 3 and 4 kidney disease.
2. Calories provide energy and help you repair and maintain body tissues. Your food contains calories from fat, protein and carbohydrate. Proteins are limited in the predialysis diet for kidney disease, and so is sodium. You have to learn to eat more calories but not more protein.
3. Carbohydrates play into the overall amount of food that you eat as well as affecting those with diabetes. You will likely fill up the extra room on your plate (that is available because of a smaller portion of meat) with carbohydrate. Be sure to include more unprocessed and whole grain carbohydrates like whole grain breads and brown rice. As your kidney disease progresses, you should limit your intake of whole wheat products, but if you are not on a phosphorus or potassium restriction you can still eat them without limits. Even if you are on a potassium restriction, use ½ and ½ of regular and whole wheat products – that way you still get the fiber but less of the potassium. Eat more raw or whole unprocessed vegetables and fruits as well. The fiber will slow the absorption and make you feel full for longer. The less the foods are processed, the more of the nutrients they retain and provide to your body.
4. Proteins are needed by your body to repair tissue and make different hormones for your body to use in processes in your organs. In the process of using proteins, your body produces waste products and those are difficult for your kidneys to process. This is why you should limit your protein intake during predialysis kidney disease. You can limit your protein to about 45 – 75 gm per day. 3 ounces of meat is about 21 gm of protein, so eating 3 ounces of meat 3 times per day fits in that allowance. 3 ounces of meat is about the size of a deck of cards.

5. Sodium is the other culprit you must manage to lower your blood pressure and help your kidneys cope. Salt is associated with higher blood pressure and you want to keep your blood pressure as low as possible during the predialysis phase of kidney disease to hopefully slow the progression of kidney disease. Reducing the amount of sodium in the food you eat will help your kidneys tremendously. Using spices and herbs that are low or no sodium instead of salt is a good first step, as well as not using a salt shaker on your food. Food might taste bland at first, but your tastebuds will adjust and you will soon find the food to be very tasty.
6. Phosphorus may be a concern for you, and you need to realize almost all foods contain some amount of phosphorus. Your kidneys will have a hard time with too much phosphorus, but you can take phosphate binders to reduce the amount you absorb and help keep your blood levels low. Rich sources of phosphorous are milk products, nuts, beer, chocolate, kidney beans, lentils and dark colored soft drinks.

STAGE 3 AND 4 REQUIREMENTS FOR PRE-DIALYSIS KIDNEY DISEASE

You may be wondering why you need a pre-dialysis meal plan or recipes in the first place. It's almost too frustrating to imagine all the restrictions you have to manage. But with a well thought out plan, you can have good meals that you enjoy.

Because your kidneys are so intimately involved in your health, living without them is unimaginable. Until less than 50 years ago, people who reached end stage renal disease died because medical doctors could not help them. But now, you have a lot of options.

First and foremost, you can follow a predialysis diet plan. Based on which stage you are in, you can follow a slightly different meal plan to guide you down the right path. Your body's needs in each stage are changing and your diet can be adjusted to meet those needs.

There are 5 different stages in kidney deterioration. The dietary needs at different stages of disease advancement are different. As kidney disease progresses from stage 1 to stage 5, the amount of protein that you are allowed to eat becomes smaller. In contrast, those who are at the end stage of the renal disease should increase their protein intake when on dialysis. It can be difficult to know when to change your amount of protein, but discussions with your nephrologist will help.

Protein Needs:

In a stage 3 or 4 kidney disease diet for pre-dialysis, most doctors recommend something in the range of 40-50 gm of protein per day. Reducing your overall intake of protein at this stage is crucial because it is the way to preserve your kidney function.

Sodium Needs:

Eating a lower sodium diet is also crucial to preserve kidney function. You are at higher risk of heart problems and may already be taking medication to lower blood pressure. Eating between 1,500 – 2,000 miligrams of sodium per day is ideal. You may not make it every day, but if you target lower sodium foods you will get there. Especially if you eat more of the raw and unprocessed foods.

Fluid Needs:

Your fluid needs are dependent on how well your kidneys are working. You should stay away from dark colored sodas to reduce the amount of potassium and phosphorus you take in. Otherwise, as long as you are still producing urine, your body and kidneys are working well enough and you should not have to be on a fluid restriction. Verify with your physician if you are confused.

HOW TO CALCULATE YOUR MEALS FOR THE DAY

In buying a recipe book, you are going to find many meals that you can create that are going to work for your particular needs. You may or may not have information about how the renal diet meal plan should be put together. We have a pre-done meal plan with weekly updates on the recipes on our website at www.renaldiethq.com if you are interested in having it done for you.

Otherwise, you can start by thinking about what you need to eat every day. Think about the way you normally eat, or what feels normal to you as far as a pattern. Are you a small meals eater or do you eat 3 large meals, or even less? Is your biggest meal your breakfast or your supper? The pattern that you should follow is an inverted pyramid, where you eat more early in the day and less as the day goes on. Almost the inverse of what you are probably used to. Whatever you do now, go ahead and lay it out. Plan out what your day will be as far as eating.

Now, we need to figure out how many calories you need in a day. To calculate your calorie needs (estimated), you need to start with your weight.

1. If you are overweight (enter your weight and height into a BMI calculator on line and see if it puts you in the overweight or obese range), you need to take your weight in kilograms (to find your weight in kilograms, take your weight in pounds and divide by 2.2) and multiply it by 25.
    a. If you weigh 200 pounds, then your weight in kilograms is 90.9.
    b. Take 90.9 X 25 = 2,273 calories per day to maintain your weight. Round that number up or down – I would use 2, 200 calories as my goal for the day.
2. If you are not overweight, you should take your weight in kilograms (to find your weight in kilograms, take your weight in pounds and divide by 2.2) and multiply by 35 to get your daily calorie needs.
    a. If you weigh 150 pounds, then your weight in kilograms is 68.18.
    b. Take 68.18 X 35 = 2,386 calories per day to maintain your weight. Round that up or down – probably around 2,400 claories for the day as a goal.
3. Now you take that amount you got in either #1 or #2 and divide it up for the day. If you normally eat 3 meals and no snacks, then divide it up in relation to your meals (more for your large meals, less for your smaller meals).
4. If you have 2,400 calories for the day, and you are used to eating 3 meals and a snack, then you might figure calories for each meal as:
    a. Breakfast – 500 calories (a light breakfast)
    b. Lunch – 800 calories
    c. Supper – 800 calories
    d. Evening snack – 300 calories
5. What goes in each meal? Now that you know calories, you need to divide up your protein for the day. It's easy enough to do – either your doctor told you how much to eat or you can aim for .6 - .8 gm of protein per kilogram of body weight.

a. In our example above, for a weight of 68.18 kilograms, the amount of protein to eat for the day is between 40.9 (0.6 X 68.18) and 54.5 (0.8 X 68.18). 40 – 54 gm of protein per day.

b. How much protein is in something? Read the label. Also, if you remember that a 3 ounce portion of meat looks about like the size of a deck of cards. (or the palm of your hand). That amount of protein is 21 grams. So you could eat 3 ounces of protein 2 times per day and you will get your amount you need.

c. Realize that most food does have protein in it, so aiming for the low end of the protein as your animal protein source, you will also get protein in vegetables and starches.

d. For more detailed information on calculating all the elements of your stage 3-4 kidney diet, please see my other book entitled: *Create Your Own Kidney Diet: Build A Meal Pattern For Stage 3 or 4 Kidney Disease* (available on Amazon)

6. For amounts of carbohydrate to eat – I would recommend that you place your portion on meat as ¼ of your meal, your starch as ¼ of your meal and your vegetables as ½ of your meal. Complement the meal with a slice of whole grain or white bread as instructed by your dietitian or doctor.

7. Potatoes are a very popular starch that a lot of people eat. You should consider limiting potatoes (not eliminating them) to once or twice a week. You can eat pasta and rice instead. Brown rice can be purchased pre-cooked so you don't even have to wait for it to be done.

8. Eat more fruits and vegetables that are low potassium foods. Look for – apples, blackberries, grapes, mandarin oranges, peaches, pineapple, and strawberries in the fruit category. Eat more asparagus, green or wax beans, cucumbers, mushrooms, peppers, lettuce and zucchini.

9. Plan your day out – start with the main food item – usually a protein. Pick your protein and amount of ounces for each meal. Then choose your sides – choose a starch, a vegetable and a fruit if possible. Look at calories and if you can add a piece of bread with butter, go ahead, but if it doesn't fit – save it for a snack.

a. In our example, you might choose lunch to be 800 calories. Then you pick an entrée with about 3 ounces of meat (perhaps a sandwich). Add your bread and a salad with dressing. Add toppings to the sandwich of lettuce and mayonnaise. Look at how many calories that would be for you and add accordingly – either some fruit or another tablespoon of dressing.

HOW YOU FEEL, YOUR LIMITATIONS

The importance of a renal diet cannot be understated. You will feel completely different once you start following a kidney diet plan that meets your needs without making you feel worse. It is a serious matter when you are talking about how to eat and what to eat. You need to know how the nutrients affect your body.

The benefits of following a renal diet menu are enormous. First of all, you manage your kidney disease. No more feeling so awful or wondering if food is ok for you – you have the ability to choose the items you need for nourishment and have the information about how they can affect your body.

Second, you are helping your kidney disease to slow down. Preventing renal failure from progressing further is a huge victory for you. You can slow or stop the way your kidneys are deteriorating just by eating a balanced diet and following a meal plan.

Next, you can manage certain electrolytes and and protein which control the protein waste and phosphorus in your blood. Your body can stay strong while only receiving the foods and nutrition that your body needs.

Balancing a diet and managing your health are going to make you feel better even if you can't have everything you want.

For predialysis meal planning, it is important to note that many people don't necessarily have a phosphorus or potassium restriction – mainly just a protein and sodium limit. That means that you can eat a little more tomato and other high potassium foods. Even if you have a limitation, you can eat some of the foods some of the time.

Eating the right amount of foods is key as well. Sometimes you can become so restricted that you are not eating enough out of fear of hurting your kidneys further. It's important to find the balance. The two most important nutrients are sodium and protein, so if you are controlling those and you are doing well with limiting the progression of kidney disease, then let your diet breathe a little. Don't go overboard, but don't be so restrictive that you can't eat anything you enjoy.

High sodium foods are things like canned vegetables and soups. In this recipe book, we review ways to make beef, chicken and vegetable broth from stock, and that will help you make a low sodium soup. You will get used to the taste of less sodium, but only if you follow the diet. Making more food from home is the best place to start, and a cook book will get you there quickly.

Other tips on lowering sodium include using whole foods instead of more processed ones and using less condiments. Many times we don't even think to read the label on the ketchup bottle, but it contains a great deal of sugar and some sodium. Almost all processed foods contain a certain amount of sodium, and they all add up. Add portion size control to that mix, and you are certain to lower your sodium intake.

ABOUT THE NUTRITIONAL ANALYSIS

To help you manage your kidney diet and understand more about the food in this book, we have provided nutritional information on each recipe in a per serving amount. I made every effort to make sure it is up to date and accurate, but because of the many foods that are involved and variability, you should consider the information as approximate values.

Each nutritional analysis is based on a single serving of said recipe, and only considers the listed ingredients. When I analyzed the recipes, I used the lowest sodium ingredients available when possible. For example, the broth in all the soup recipes is assumed to be the broth from our recipe book which is very low sodium.

Meats and chicken are analyzed as cooked and without the skin or extra fat. Ground beef is assumed to be a 90/10 Lean version. Most of the recipes where oil is used, you will find olive oil. I feel it is the healthiest oil, but you can use canola, corn, or other heart healthy unsaturated oils. And because products come and go, I tried to use the most generic terminology, like "low-fat" or "fat-free" instead of identifiying a specific brand.

Also, in the recipes, I used g for grams and mg for milligrams.

BREAKFAST ITEMS

Cinnamon Oatmeal Breakfast Bars

Applesauce Nut Muffins

Fruit Salad with Yogurt and Honey

Savory Frittata

Yummy Pancakes with Strawberry Compote

CINNAMON OATMEAL BREAKFAST BARS

CINNAMON OATMEAL BREAKFAST BARS

Serves: 12   Portion Size: 1 Square

Ingredients:

3 cups	Old Fashioned Oats
1 cup	Seedless Raisins
2 tsp	Baking Powder
2 tsp	Ground Cinnamon
½ cup	Plain Nonfat Yogurt
½ cup	Skim Milk
2 Tbsp	Honey
½ cup	Sweetened Applesauce
2 each	Whole Eggs
¼ cup	Canola Oil
2 tsp	Vanilla Extract
2 Tbsp	Brown Sugar

Instructions:

Make these up in advance, and eat them for breakfast over the period of the week.

Preheat oven to 350°. Combine oats, raisins and baking powder and 1 ½ teaspoons cinnamon in a large bowl. In another bowl, mix together nonfat yogurt, skim milk, honey, apple sauce, eggs, oil, and vanilla extract until well mixed.

Add liquid to dry ingredients and stir thoroughly.

Pour this mixture into a lightly oiled 8 in. square baking dish. Sprinkle top with brown sugar and remaining ½ teaspoon of cinnamon. Bake for 30 to 35 minutes. A toothpick inserted in the middle should come out clean. Allow to cool for 15 to 20 minutes before cutting into 12 squares. (Approx 2.5 in by 2 in each)

Nutritional information per serving:

Calories: 182.4 , Protein: 3.9 g, Carbohydrate: 29.1 g, Dietary Fiber: 1.8 g, Total Fat: 6.3 g, Saturated Fat: .8 g, Cholesterol: 35.7 mg, Calcium: 103.1 mg, Phosphorus: 119.2 mg, Potassium: 215.7 mg, Sodium: 110.7 mg

APPLESAUCE NUT MUFFINS

Serves: 12   Portion Size: 1 muffin

Ingredients:

3 Tbsp	Canola Oil
½ cup	Packed Brown Sugar
1 each	Egg
1 cup	Sweetened Applesauce
¾ cup	Peeled and Sliced Apple
1 cup	Whole Wheat Flour
½ cup	White Wheat Flour
1 tsp	Salt
½ tsp	Baking Soda
½ tsp	Baking Powder
¼ cup	Chopped Walnuts
½ tsp	Ground Nutmeg
½ tsp	Ground Cinnamon
¾ tsp	Ground Allspice

Instructions:

Preheat oven to 400°. In a large mixing bowl, beat together the oil, brown sugar, and egg until smooth. Stir in applesauce and finely diced apples. In a separate bowl, mix together the dry ingredients, spices and nuts. Stir into the applesauce mixture, just until moistened. Do not over mix. Spray 12 muffin cups with cooking oil spray, fill, and bake for 15 to 18 minutes. Let muffins cool in the pan for 5 minutes. Remove from pan and cool on a rack.

Make muffins by the dozen to freeze, take them out at night for use the next morning. Instead of oiling the muffin pans, you can simply use paper muffin cups.

Nutritional information per serving:

Calories: 159.3, Protein: 2.8 g, Carbohydrate: 25.3 g, Dietary Fiber: 1.9 g, Total Fat: 5.8 g, Saturated Fat: .615 g, Cholesterol: 17.6 mg, Phosphorus: 63.8 mg, Potassium: 98.5 mg, Sodium: 179.2 mg

FRUIT SALAD WITH YOGURT AND HONEY

Serves: 6   Portion Size: 1/6 Of Mixture

Ingredients:

¾ cup	Nonfat Plain Yogurt
2 Tbsp	Honey
½ tsp	Vanilla Extract
½ cup	Chopped Apples
¾ cup	Grapes
1 each	Asian Pear
½ cup	Sliced Banana
1 Tbsp	Lemon Juice
¼ cup	Almonds
½ ounce	Seedless Raisins

Instructions:

Stir together the yogurt, honey, and vanilla until smooth. Chop apples into small pieces, and grapes cut in half. Also dice the pear and slice the banana. Prepare fruit and toss together in a bowl. Sprinkle fruit with lemon juice. Combine with yogurt mixture, divide into serving bowls, and top with nuts and raisins.

Nutritional information per serving:

Calories: 114.1, Protein: 3.4 g, Carbohydrate: 19.7 g, Dietary Fiber: 2.2 g, Total Fat: 3.257 g, Saturated Fat: .303 g, Cholesterol: .613 mg, Phosphorus: 86.4 mg, Potassium: 247.9 mg, Sodium: 25.2 mg

SAVORY FRITTATA

SERVES: 4   PORTION SIZE: 1/4TH OF 8 INCH PIE PAN

Ingredients:

2 cups	Spinach Leaves, Raw
2 Tbsp	Water
1 Tbsp	Olive Oil
½ cup	Onion, Chopped, Raw
1 tsp	Minced Garlic
1 cup	Red Pepper, Sliced, Raw
¼ cup	Grated Parmesan Cheese, Reduced Fat
1 dash	Black Pepper
8 each	Egg Whites
4 each	Whole Eggs

Instructions:

Place oven rack in center of oven and preheat broiler. Dice onion and cut pepper into bite-size pieces. To prepare greens, remove tough centers and stems and chop leaves into bite-size pieces. In a nonstick, ovenproof skillet, heat olive oil and sauté onion and garlic until golden. Add red pepper and sauté briefly. Add greens and a splash of water just enough to wilt the greens. Cover pan and allow the spinach greens to steam until tender, 5 to 10 minutes. The denser the leaf the more cooking is needed. Whisk whole eggs and egg whites with 2 tablespoons water. Add pepper. Put vegetables in the bottom of the pie pan.

Remove lid and pour egg mixture evenly over vegetables. Sprinkle with Parmesan cheese. Broil just until eggs are set, about 6 to 8 minutes. Remove, cut into wedges, and serve with roasted vegetables if desired.

You can also make this frittata completely on top of the stove. Once you add the eggs, turn the heat down very low, cover skillet, and cook until eggs are set.

Nutritional information per serving:

Calories: 169, Protein: 15.7 g, Carbohydrate: 5 g, Dietary Fiber: 1.2 g, Total Fat: 9.9 g, Saturated Fat: 2.9 g, Cholesterol: 217 mg, Phosphorus: 171.2 mg, Potassium: 347.1 mg, Sodium: 289.1 mg

YUMMY PANCAKES WITH STRAWBERRY COMPOTE

Serves: 6   Portion Size: 2 pancakes

Ingredients:

1 ½ cup	Strawberries, Frozen, Unsweetened
1 Tbsp	Cornstarch
½ cup	Apple Juice
1 Tbsp	Lemon Juice
½ cup	Cream of Wheat, Dry
½ cup	Flour, All-Purpose
1 Tbsp	Sugar
1 Tbsp	Baking Powder
¾ cup	Fat Free Milk
1 each	Whole Egg
1 Tbsp	Olive Oil
1 each	Banana, Sliced
¼ cup	Walnuts, Chopped

Instructions:

For the compote: in a medium saucepan, combine cornstarch, sugar, and salt. Blend in cold juice and mix well. Add strawberries and heat over medium heat until thickened and bubbly. Remove from heat and add lemon juice mixing well.

For the pancakes: Mix dry ingredients together in a bowl. In a separate bowl combine milk, egg, banana and oil. Stir into dry ingredients just until blended and batter is lumpy. Let stand 10 minutes and then stir in walnuts.

Heat a lightly greased skillet or griddle over medium high heat. Pour batter by 1/4 cupfuls onto pan. Turn when the first bubbles break; cook until second side is golden brown. Serve with warm strawberry compote. Nutritional does not include syrup.

Nutritional information per serving:

Calories: 228, Protein: 5.9 g, Carbohydrate: 37.3 g, Dietary Fiber: 2.8 g, Total Fat: 6.8 g, Saturated Fat: 1 g, Cholesterol: 35.9 mg, Phosphorus: 154.4 mg, Potassium: 289.1 mg, Sodium: 273.5 mg

BEEF ENTREES

Strip Steaks with Mango Peach Salsa

Asian Beef Noodle Salad

Beef Tips with Mushroom Gravy

Chipotle Barbecue Burger with Slaw

Hamburger Stroganoff

Meatloaf

Orange Teriyaki Beef with Noodles

Patty Melt with Grilled Onions

Shepherd's Pie

STRIP STEAKS WITH MANGO PEACH SALSA

STRIP STEAKS WITH MANGO PEACH SALSA

Serves: 4   Portion Size: 2 ½ ounce Steak + Salsa

Ingredients:

¼ cup	Chopped Red Bell Pepper
2 Tbsp	Diced Green Chilies
½ tsp	Ground Ginger
4 Tbsp	Peach Preserves
1 ounce	Lime Juice
¾ cup	Peeled and Sliced Mango
10 ounces	Beef Strip Steak
1 Tbsp	Onion Powder
1 tsp	Ground Thyme
1 tsp	Ground Allspice
1 tsp	Black Pepper
¼ tsp	Ground Cinnamon
¼ tsp	Red or Cayenne Pepper

Instructions:

Salsa: Mix the red bell pepper, chilies, and ginger in a medium bowl. Stir in peach preserves, lime juice and mango. You can use frozen mango if you like.

Steaks: Set oven control to broil. Mix together the onion powder, thyme, allspice, black pepper, ground cinnamon, and cayenne pepper. Rub seasoning into meat.

Place on rack in broiler pan. Broil with tops 4 to 6 inches from heat for 6 to 10 minutes, turning once until desired doneness. Serve topped with salsa.

Nutritional information per serving:

Calories: 209.4, Protein: 15.6 g, Carbohydrate: 23.2 g, Dietary Fiber: 2 g, Total Fat: 6.12 g, Saturated Fat: 2.2 g, Cholesterol: 40.4 mg, Phosphorus: 158.5 mg, Potassium: 388 mg, Sodium: 83.3 mg

ASIAN BEEF NOODLE SALAD

Serves:	6	Portion Size:	1/6 Of Recipe

Ingredients:

1 Tbsp	Smooth Peanut Butter
4 Tbsp	Reduced Sodium Soy Sauce
½ ounce	Lime Juice
¼ tsp	Cayenne Pepper
4 Tbsp	Fresh Peppermint
2 Tbsp	Red Wine Vinegar
6 ounces	Sliced Beef Sirloin
1 Tbsp	Sesame Oil
2 cup	Peeled and Sliced Cucumber
1 cup	Grated Carrots
1 cup	Chopped Onions
1/8 cup	Dry Roasted Peanuts, Without Salt
2 Tbsp	Sesame Seeds
12 ounces	Linguine Noodles, Dry

Instructions:

In a medium bowl, whisk together peanut butter, 2 tablespoons soy sauce, lime juice, cayenne pepper and mint ingredients. Set aside. Cook noodles according to package directions, omitting salt; drain and rinse under cold water to cool. In a medium bowl, whisk together soy sauce and rice wine vinegar. Add beef and toss to coat. Add the sesame oil and a generous amount of cooking spray to a large sauté pan or wok over high heat. Stir fry beef in batches; set aside to cool slightly. In a large salad bowl, toss remaining ingredients, except sesame seeds, with cooled noodles. Drizzle the dressing over the salad and toss to coat. Arrange 6 portions of the salad on salad plates and top with a portion of beef. Garnish with toasted sesame seeds.

Nutritional information per serving:

Calories: 380, Protein: 19.2 g, Carbohydrate: 49.9 g, Dietary Fiber: 3.8 g, Total Fat: 11.4 g, Saturated Fat: 2.585 g, Cholesterol: 19 mg, Phosphorus: 257.3 mg, Potassium: 476.3 mg, Sodium: 407.7 mg

BEEF TIPS WITH MUSHROOM GRAVY

Serves: 4   Portion Size: 3 ½ ounce steak

Ingredients:

12 ounces	Beef Tenderloin
½ cup	Mushrooms Slices
1 cup	Low Sodium Beef Broth (pg. 96)
1 Tbsp	Cornstarch
½ tsp	Salt
¼ tsp	Black Pepper

Instructions:

Cut beef into small pieces of 1 to 2 ounces. Coat a large nonstick skillet with cooking spray over high heat. Add beef tips to skillet and sauté for 5 to 6 minutes or until browned well. Remove beef from pan and set aside. Cover beef. Add mushrooms to pan and sauté for 4 to 5 minutes. In a small bowl, whisk together broth and cornstarch. Pour over mushrooms and bring to a boil, scraping browned bits off from the bottom of the pan. Reduce heat and simmer for 2 minutes. Stir in salt and pepper. Return beef tips and any juice and stir into gravy mixture.

Nutritional information per serving:

Calories: 230.3 , Protein: 18 g, Carbohydrate: 2.6 g, Dietary Fiber: .138 g, Total Fat: 16.1 g, Saturated Fat: 6.45 g, Cholesterol: 57.8 mg, Phosphorus: 180.8 mg, Potassium: 336.3 mg, Sodium: 351.9 mg

CHIPOTLE BARBEQUE BURGER WITH SLAW

Serves: 4   Portion Size: 2 ounce Burger, ½ c slaw + Bun

Ingredients:

1 Tbsp	Barbeque Sauce
1 Tbsp	Chili Sauce
1 tsp	Minced Garlic
8 ounces	93-95% Lean Ground Beef
1 each	Whole Egg
2 cups	Shredded Green Cabbage
1 Tbsp	Reduced Fat Mayonnaise
1 Tbsp	Reduced Fat Sour Cream
1 tsp	Sugar
1 tsp	Cider Vinegar
¼ tsp	Black Pepper
4 each	Hamburger Bun, White
½ cup	Old Fashioned Oatmeal, Dry

Instructions:

Combine cabbage and mayonnaise, sour cream, sugar, vinegar, salt, and pepper in a large bowl; toss well. Set aside to let ingredients combine.

Combine oatmeal, barbecue sauce, chili sauce, garlic, ground beef, and large egg ingredients. Divide mixture into 4 equal portions, shaping each into a ½ inch-thick patty.

Heat a large nonstick skillet over medium-high heat. Coat pan with cooking spray. Add patties to pan; cook for 4 minutes on each side or until a meat thermometer registers 160°. Place 1 patty on bottom half of each bun; top each serving with ½ cup coleslaw mixture and top half of bun.

Nutritional information per serving:

Calories: 292.4 , Protein: 18 g, Carbohydrate: 28.4 g, Dietary Fiber: 2.5 g, Total Fat: 10.1 g, Saturated Fat: 3.5 g, Cholesterol: 92.2 mg, Phosphorus: 195.2 mg, Potassium: 300.8 mg, Sodium: 375.1 mg

HAMBURGER STROGANOFF

Serves: 6   Portion Size: 1/3 c Stroganoff + ¾ c Pasta

Ingredients:

10 ounces   Egg Noodles, Dry
1 tsp   Olive Oil
10 ounces   93-95% Lean Ground Beef
1 cup   Chopped Onions
1 tsp   Minced Garlic
8 ounces   Sliced Mushrooms
2 Tbsp   All Purpose Flour
1 cup   Low Sodium Beef Broth (pg. 96)
½ tsp   Salt
1/8 tsp   Black Pepper
6 ounces   Reduced Fat Sour Cream
½ ounce   Dry Sherry
1 Tbsp   Dried Parsley

Instructions:

Cook pasta according to package directions, omitting salt and fat. Drain and rinse under cold water; drain.

Heat oil in a large nonstick skillet over medium-high heat. Add beef to pan; cook 4 minutes or until browned, stirring to crumble. Add onion, garlic, and mushrooms to pan; cook 4 minutes or until most of liquid evaporates, stirring frequently. Sprinkle with flour; cook 1 minute, stirring constantly. Stir in broth; bring to a boil. Reduce heat, and simmer 1 minute or until slightly thick. Stir in salt and pepper.

Remove from heat. Stir in sour cream and sherry. Serve over pasta. Sprinkle with parsley.

Nutritional information per serving:

Calories: 343, Protein: 20.8 g, Carbohydrate: 42.9 g, Dietary Fiber: 3 g, Total Fat: 9.5 g, Saturated Fat: 4.281 g, Cholesterol: 78.5 mg, Phosphorus: 280.4 mg, Potassium: 474.2 mg, Sodium: 429.5 mg

MEATLOAF

Serves:	8	Portion Size:	1 Slice

Ingredients:

¾ cup	Old Fashioned Oatmeal, Dry
¼ cup	Lowfat Plain Yogurt
16 ounces	93-95% Lean Ground Beef
¾ cup	Chopped Onions
1 stalk	Chopped Celery
½ cup	Chopped Carrots
¼ cup	Fat Free Egg Substitute
1 Tbsp	Capers
1 Tbsp	Lemon Juice
½ tsp	Ground Thyme
¼ tsp	Black Pepper
½ tsp	Garlic Powder

Instructions:

Preheat oven to 375°F. Lightly spray a loaf baking pan with cooking spray. Set aside. Chop the onion, chop the celery, and shred the carrots.

In a large bowl, stir together the oatmeal and yogurt. Let stand for 5 minutes. Add the remaining ingredients after 5 minutes and combine using your hands or a spoon. Shape into a loaf of that 8 x 5" and place in the baking pan. Bake for about an hour and 15 minutes, or until the meatloaf registers 165°F on an instant read thermometer and is no longer pink in the center. Remove from the oven and let stand for 5 to 10 minutes. Cut into 8 slices, one slice per serving.

Nutritional information per serving:

Calories: 147.7, Protein: 13.7 g, Carbohydrate: 8.5 g, Dietary Fiber: 1.5 g, Total Fat: 6.2 g, Saturated Fat: 2.451 g, Cholesterol: 36.9 mg, Phosphorus: 160.4 mg, Potassium: 305.1 mg, Sodium: 100.4 mg

ORANGE TERIYAKI BEEF WITH NOODLES

Serves: 4   Portion Size: ¼ Of Recipe

Ingredients:

9 oz	Beef Sirloin
1 Tbsp	Reduced Sodium Teriyaki Sauce
2 Tbsp	Orange Marmalade
¼ tsp	Cayenne Pepper
1 cup	Egg Noodles
1 ½ cups	Snow Peas
2 ½ cups	Low Sodium Beef Broth (pg. 96)

Instructions:

Cut beef into thin strips prior to cooking. Spray a 12-inch skillet with cooking spray; heat over medium-high heat. Cook beef in skillet for 4 minutes, stirring occasionally, until brown. Remove beef from skillet; keep warm.

Add beef broth, teriyaki, marmalade, and cayenne pepper to skillet. Heat to boiling. Stir in pea pods and noodles; reduce heat to medium. Cover and cook about 5 minutes or until noodles are tender. Stir in beef. Cook uncovered 2 to 3 minutes or until sauce is slightly thickened.

Nutritional information per serving:

Calories: 203, Protein: 15.2 g, Carbohydrate: 15.9 g, Dietary Fiber: 1.032 g, Total Fat: 8.5 g, Saturated Fat: 3.395 g, Cholesterol: 38 mg, Phosphorus: 161.4 mg, Potassium: 286 mg, Sodium: 110.6 mg

PATTY MELT WITH GRILLED ONIONS

Serves: 4   Portion Size: 1 Sandwich

Ingredients:

1 cup	Sliced Vidalia Onions
1 Tbsp	Balsamic Vinegar
8 ounces	93-95% Lean Ground Beef
¼ tsp	Black Pepper
3 Tbsp	Dijon Mustard
½ cup	Shredded Mozzarella Cheese
4 Slices	Reduced Calorie White Bread

Instructions:

Arrange onion slices on a plate. Drizzle vinegar over onion slices. Heat a large grill pan over medium heat. Coat pan with cooking spray. Add onion to pan; cover and cook 3 minutes on each side. Remove from pan; cover and keep warm.

Heat pan over medium-high heat. Coat pan with cooking spray. Divide beef into 4 equal portions, shaping each into a thin patty. Sprinkle patties evenly with pepper. Add patties to pan; cook 2 minutes on each side or until done.

Spread about 2 teaspoons Dijon mustard over 4 bread slices; layer each slice with 2 tablespoons cheese, 1 patty, 2 onion slices.

Heat pan over medium heat. Coat pan with cooking spray. Add sandwiches to pan. Cook 3 minutes on low heat or until bread is toasted and cheese is melted.

Nutritional information per serving:

Calories: 226.2, Protein: 18.1 g, Carbohydrate: 16.9 g, Dietary Fiber: 2.7 g, Total Fat: 10 g, Saturated Fat: 3.4 g, Cholesterol: 42.3 mg, Phosphorus: 225 mg, Potassium: 273.8 mg, Sodium: 297.8 mg

SHEPHARDS PIE

Serves: 4   Portion Size: ¾ cup

Ingredients:

1 cup	White Rice (not instant), uncooked
2 cups	Low Sodium Chicken Stock (pg. 95)
½ cup	Picante Sauce
3 ounces	Water
1 lbsp	Ground Cumin
2 Tbsp	Sugar
1 cup	Canned Red Kidney Beans
½ cup	Shredded Reduced Fat Cheddar Cheese
10 ounces	93-95% Lean Ground Beef

Instructions:

Cook rice according to package, omitting salt and using chicken stock instead of water for liquid.

Rinse canned kidney beans thoroughly, to reduce sodium content. Cook beef in a large nonstick skillet over medium-high heat until browned, stirring to crumble. Stir in picante sauce, water, cumin, sugar, and beans; bring to a boil. Reduce heat; simmer until mixture thickens (about 5 minutes).

Remove from heat. Spoon cooked rice over meat mixture, and sprinkle with cheese. Cover and let stand 2 minutes or until cheese melts.

Nutritional information per serving:

Calories: 395.9, Protein: 23.4 g, Carbohydrate: 56.7 g, Dietary Fiber: 5.237 g, Total Fat: 10.4 g, Saturated Fat: 4.6 g, Cholesterol: 53.4 mg, Phosphorus: 317.5 mg, Potassium: 500.4 mg, Sodium: 412.8 mg

PORK ENTREES

Pork Chops with Cranberry Glaze

Breaded Pork Cutlet

Caramel Pork

Moroccan Pork with Caramelized Radicchio

Pan-fried Pork Chop with Gravy

Pork Chops Oregano

Pork Stir-fry

Pork Tenderloin Medallions with Sauce

Spicy Sweet and Sour Pork

PORK CHOPS WITH CRANBERRY GLAZE

PORK CHOPS WITH CRANBERRY GLAZE

Serves: 4   Portion Size: 3 ounce Chop

Ingredients:

12 ounces	Lean Pork Chops, With Bone
1 tsp	Minced Garlic
¼ tsp	Salt
½ tsp	Black Pepper
1 tsp	Olive Oil
1 cup	Sliced Red Onions
1 Tbsp	Honey
½ cup	Balsamic Vinegar
3 ounces	Water
1/3 cup	Dried Cranberries

Instructions:

Season pork chops well with garlic, salt and pepper. Add oil to a large nonstick skillet over medium to high heat. Sauté chops for 6 to 8 minutes or until browned, turning once. Remove from pan and keep chops warm. Spray pan with cooking spray. Add onions and cook for 5 to 6 minutes or until they begin to caramelize. Stir in honey, balsamic vinegar, water and cranberries and simmer for 5 to 7 minutes or until cranberries are soft and sauce takes honey glaze consistency. Pour cranberry sauce over pork chops and serve.

Nutritional information per serving:

Calories: 203.4 , Protein: 19.3 g, Carbohydrate: 20.4 g, Dietary Fiber: 1.1 g, Total Fat: 4.4 g, Saturated Fat: 1.1 g, Cholesterol: 58.7 mg, Phosphorus: 204 mg, Potassium: 398.3 mg, Sodium: 204.5 mg

BREADED PORK CUTLET

| Serves: | 4 | Portion Size: | 2-ounce Pork Cutlet |

Ingredients:

¾ cup	Plain Bread Crumbs
½ tsp	Black Pepper
½ tsp	Ground Sage
½ tsp	Ground Thyme
8 ounces	Boneless Pork Sirloin Chops
¼ cup	All Purpose Flour
3 each	Egg Whites
2 tsp	Olive Oil
1 each	Lemon, Sliced into wedges

Instructions:

Cut pork into 2 ounce portions. Combine pepper, sage, and thyme; sprinkle over both sides of pork. Place flour in a shallow dish; place egg whites in another shallow dish. Dredge pork in flour, dip in egg whites, and dredge in bread crumbs. Heat oil in a large nonstick skillet over medium-high heat. Add pork to pan. Cook 2 ½ minutes or until lightly browned. Lightly coat surface of chops with cooking spray; turn chops over. Cook 2 ½ minutes or until done. Serve with lemon wedges.

Nutritional information per serving:

Calories: 214.2, Protein: 18.2 g, Carbohydrate: 21.1 g, Dietary Fiber: 1.2 g, Total Fat: 5.8 g, Saturated Fat: 1.4 g, Cholesterol: 35.7 mg, Phosphorus: 170.1 mg, Potassium: 303.9 mg, Sodium: 218.7 mg

CARAMEL PORK

Serves: 4   Portion Size: ½ c Pork + ½ cup Rice

Ingredients:

8 ounces	Water
¾ cup	White Rice (not instant), Dry
½ cup	Frozen Peas
1 Tbsp	Rice Vinegar
9 ounces	Pork Tenderloin
½ cup	Chopped Onions
1 Tbsp	Minced Garlic
½ cup	Low Sodium Chicken Stock (pg. 95)
1/8 cup	Brown Sugar
1 Tbsp	Low Sodium Soy Sauce
1 tsp	Ground Ginger
½ tsp	Spice, Red Pepper
1 each	Lime, Sliced into wedges

Instructions:

Combine 1 cup water, and rice in a small saucepan; bring to a boil. Cover, reduce heat, and simmer 15 minutes; remove from heat. Let stand 10 minutes; gently stir in peas and vinegar.

Heat a medium skillet over high heat. Coat pan with cooking spray. Add pork; sauté 5 minutes. Add onion and garlic; stir-fry 2 minutes. Stir in chicken stock, brown sugar, soy sauce, ground ginger, and red pepper, then bring to a boil. Reduce heat; simmer 5 minutes or until slightly thick. Spoon ½ cup rice on each of 4 plates; top each serving with ½ cup pork mixture. Serve with lime wedges.

Nutritional information per serving:

Calories: 265.7, Protein: 18.4 g, Carbohydrate: 42.7 g, Dietary Fiber: 2.5 g, Total Fat: 2.1 g, Saturated Fat: .6 g, Cholesterol: 41.5 mg, Phosphorus: 253.2 mg, Potassium: 453.8 mg, Sodium: 200.7 mg

MOROCCAN PORK WITH CARAMALIZED RADICCHIO

Serves: 4   Portion Size: 3 ounce Pork Chop

Ingredients:

1 tsp	Ground Cumin
1 tsp	Paprika
¼ tsp	Cayenne Pepper
¼ tsp	Ground Cinnamon
¼ tsp	Dry Mustard
12 ounces	Boneless Lean Pork Chops
2 tsp	Olive Oil
2 cups	Radicchio
1 tsp	Sugar
½ tsp	Salt
¼ tsp	Black Pepper

Instructions:

In a small bowl, combine the cumin, paprika, cayenne pepper, ground cinnamon and dry mustard. Dredge one side of each pork chop in spice mixture. Add oil and a generous amount of cooking spray to a large nonstick skillet over high heat. Place chop spice side down in the skillet. Cook for 6 minutes on each side. Remove from pan and set aside. Spray skillet generously again and add radicchio to the pan. Sauté radicchio for 2 minutes. Add sugar, salt and pepper. Sauté 5 to 6 more minutes or until radicchio begins to caramelize. Serve radicchio on top of each pork chop.

Nutritional information per serving:

Calories: 163, Protein: 19.1 g, Carbohydrate: 2.7 g, Dietary Fiber: .5 g, Total Fat: 8.0 g, Saturated Fat: 2.2 g, Cholesterol: 46.8 mg, Phosphorus: 190.2 mg, Potassium: 445.8 mg, Sodium: 334.6 mg

PAN-FRIED PORK CHOP WITH GRAVY

Serves: 4   Portion Size: 2 ½ ounce chop +1 cup Gravy

Ingredients:

¼ cup	All Purpose Flour
¼ tsp	Dried Marjoram
¼ tsp	Ground Thyme
¼ tsp	Ground Sage
10 ounces	Boneless Lean Pork Chops
1 Tbsp	Butter, No Salt Added
1 ½ cups	Lowfat Milk

Instructions:

Lightly spoon flour into a dry measuring cup; level with a knife. Place flour, dried marjoram, dried thyme, and dried rubbed sage in a shallow dish. Dredge pork in flour mixture, turning to coat; shake off excess. Reserve remaining flour mixture.

Melt butter in a large nonstick skillet coated with cooking spray over medium-high heat. Add pork to pan; cook 2 minutes on each side or until browned. Reduce heat, and cook for 10 minutes or until done, turning pork once. Remove pork from pan; keep warm.

Combine reserved flour mixture and milk in a small bowl, stirring with a whisk until blended. Add milk mixture to pan; place over medium-high heat. Bring to a boil, scraping pan to loosen browned bits. Reduce heat, and simmer 2 minutes or until slightly thickened, stirring constantly. Serve with chops.

Nutritional information per serving:

Calories: 191, Protein: 19.5 g, Carbohydrate: 10.6 g, Dietary Fiber: .2 g, Total Fat: 7.3 g, Saturated Fat: 3.2 g, Cholesterol: 46.9 mg, Phosphorus: 243.5 mg, Potassium: 448.1 mg, Sodium: 74.6 mg

PORK CHOPS OREGANO

Serves: 4   Portion Size: 3 ounce Pork Chop

Ingredients:

1 Tbsp	Olive Oil
1 each	Juice from Fresh Lemon
½ tsp	Grated Rind from Lemon
1 tsp	Ground Oregano
1 Tbsp	Minced Garlic
12 ounces	Pork Sirloin Chops
1 tsp	Black Pepper

Instructions:

Grate lemon rind and squeeze lemon for juice. Combine olive oil, lemon rind, lemon juice, oregano and garlic in an 11 x 7 inch baking dish. Add pork, turning to coat. Let stand 30 minutes, turning pork occasionally.

Preheat broiler.

Remove pork from baking dish; discard marinade. Place pork on a broiler pan coated with cooking spray. Broil 4 minutes on each side or until done.

Nutritional information per serving:

Calories: 146.8, Protein: 18.2 g, Carbohydrate: 2.2 g, Dietary Fiber: .3 g, Total Fat: 7 g, Saturated Fat: 1.7 g, Cholesterol: 53.6 mg, Phosphorus: 190.6 mg, Potassium: 347.5 mg, Sodium: 44.2 mg

PORK STIR-FRY

Serves: 4   Portion Size: ¼ Of Recipe

Ingredients:

10 ounces	Fresh Ground Pork
2 cups	Chopped Broccoli Florets
½ cup	Sliced Red Bell Pepper
1 cup	Sliced Mushrooms
½ cup	Low Sodium Chicken Stock (pg. 95)
1 Tbsp	Cornstarch
2 Tbsp	Reduced Sodium Soy Sauce
1 tsp	Minced Garlic
1 cup	Brown Rice, Uncooked

Instructions:

Cook pork in a large nonstick skillet or wok over medium to high heat for 5 to 7 minutes or until no longer pink. Drain any excess fat and remove from pan. Cook brown rice according to package directions, omitting salt and fat. Coat the pan with cooking spray. Add broccoli, sliced red bell pepper, and mushrooms and sauté for 5 to 6 minutes. Add pork back to pan. In a small bowl, whisk chicken stock, cornstarch, soy sauce, and garlic. Pour over mixture and bring to a boil. Reduce heat and simmer 2 to 3 minutes. Serve over brown rice.

Nutritional information per serving:

Calories: 399.3, Protein: 18.5 g, Carbohydrate: 43.6 g, Dietary Fiber: 3.5 g, Total Fat: 16.8 g, Saturated Fat: 5.93 g, Cholesterol: 51 mg, Phosphorus: 333.6 mg, Potassium: 609.6 mg, Sodium: 336.4 mg

PORK TENDERLOIN MEDALLIONS WITH SAUCE

Serves: 4   Portion Size: 3 Slices Plus Sauce

Ingredients:

1 Tbsp	Olive Oil
1 Tbsp	Chopped Onions
1 tsp	Minced Garlic
1 cup	Balsamic Vinegar
1 ½ tsp	Sugar
1 tsp	Dried Rosemary
1 tsp	Dijon Mustard
12 ounces	Lean Pork Tenderloin

Instructions:

Heat oil in a small saucepan over medium-high heat. Add onions and garlic; sauté 2 minutes. Add vinegar, sugar, rosemary, dijon mustard; cook until reduced to ½ cup.

Heat a large skillet over medium-high heat. Coat pan with cooking spray. Cut pork into equal 12 slices. Place pork in pan; cook 2 minutes on each side. Add balsamic reduction; cook 1 minute, turning pork to coat.

Nutritional information per serving:

Calories: 202.4, Protein: 18.3 g, Carbohydrate: 14 g, Dietary Fiber: .1 g, Total Fat: 6.5 g, Saturated Fat: 1.2 g, Cholesterol: 55.3 mg, Phosphorus: 225.2 mg, Potassium: 420.5 mg, Sodium: 86.9 mg

SPICY SWEET-AND-SOUR PORK

Serves: 4   Portion Size: 1 ¼ cup

Ingredients:

¼ cup	Slivered Almonds
10 ounces	Pork Tenderloin
2 Tbsp	Cornstarch
3 Tbsp	Low Sodium Soy Sauce
1 cup	Pineapple Chunks
¼ cup	Cider Vinegar
¼ cup	Sugar
1 Tbsp	Tabasco Sauce
1 Tbsp	Olive Oil
1 cup	Chopped Onions
1 tsp	Peeled and Sliced Ginger Root
1 tsp	Minced Garlic
1 cup	Chopped Green Pepper
¼ cup	Chopped Green Onions

Instructions:

Preheat oven to 400°. Place almonds on a baking sheet; bake at 400° for 4 minutes or until toasted. Set aside. Cut pork into three-quarter inch cubes.

While almonds cook, combine pork, 1 tablespoon cornstarch, and 1 tablespoon soy sauce; toss well to coat. Drain pineapple in a strainer over a bowl, reserving juice. Combine juice, remaining 1 tablespoon cornstarch, remaining soy sauce, vinegar, sugar, and Tabasco sauce, stirring with a whisk. Heat a large nonstick skillet over medium-high heat. Add oil to pan; swirl to coat. Add pork to pan; sauté 3 minutes, stirring frequently. Add 1 cup onion, ginger, and garlic; sauté 1 minute. Stir in pineapple and bell pepper; sauté 3 minutes, stirring frequently. Stir in vinegar mixture; bring to a boil. Cook 1 minute, stirring constantly. Sprinkle with almonds and green onions.

Nutritional information per serving:

Calories: 289.6, Protein: 18.3 g, Carbohydrate: 36.4 g, Dietary Fiber: 2.9 g, Total Fat: 8.4 g, Saturated Fat: 1.2 g, Cholesterol: 46.1 mg, Phosphorus: 244 mg, Potassium: 577 mg, Sodium: 331.6 mg

Orange and Ginger Glazed Turkey Cutlets

Tarragon Turkey Cutlet Medallions

Chicken Marsala

Chicken Penne with Tomato Sauce

Greek Lemon Chicken and Rice

Lemon Basil Chicken

Roasted Lemon Herb Turkey Breast

Salsa Turkey Meatloaf

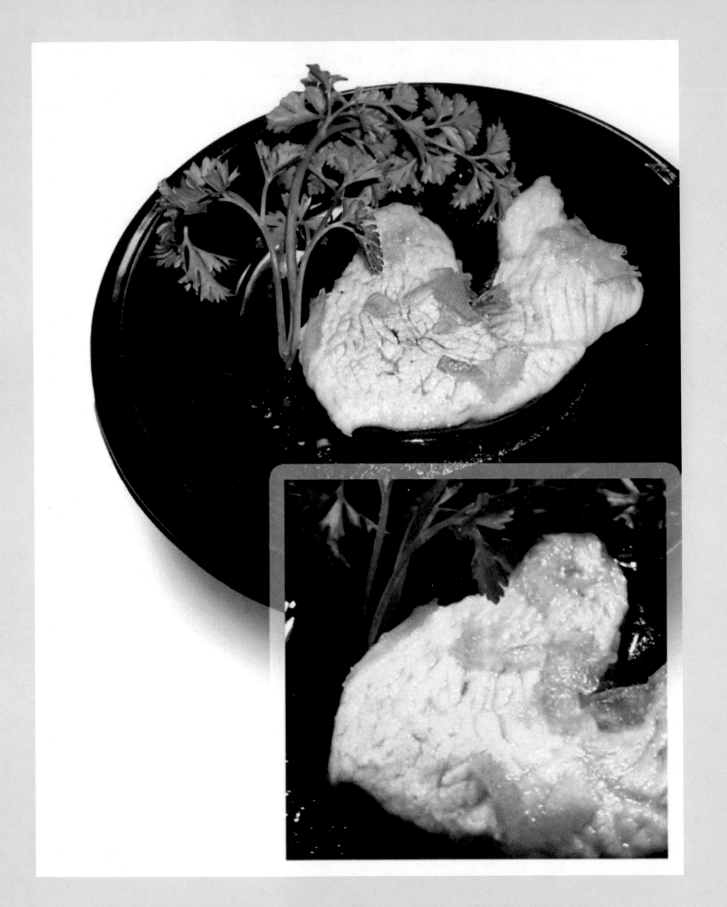

ORANGE AND GINGER GLAZED TURKEY CUTLETS

ORANGE AND GINGER GLAZED TURKEY CUTLETS

Serves: 4   Portion Size: 3 ounce Turkey Cutlet

Ingredients:

1 Tbsp	Olive Oil
12 ounces	Turkey Cutlets
1/3 cup	Orange Marmalade
½ tsp	Ground Ginger
1 tsp	Worcestershire Sauce

Instructions:

Heat the oil in a 10 inch skillet over medium heat. Cook turkey tenderloins and oil about 5 minutes or until brown on one side; turn turkey over. Stir in other ingredients; reduce heat to low. Cover and simmer 15 to 20 minutes, stirring occasionally, until sauce is thickened and juice of turkey is no longer pink when center at thickest piece is cut. Spoon sauce over turkey.

Nutritional information per serving:

Calories: 190.8, Protein: 19.1 g, Carbohydrate: 18.1 g, Dietary Fiber: .2 g, Total Fat: 4.7 g, Saturated Fat: .9 g, Cholesterol: 62.1 mg, Phosphorus: 158.7 mg Potassium: 245.4 mg, Sodium: 80.8 mg

TARRAGON TURKEY MEDALLIONS

TARRAGON TURKEY MEDALLIONS

Serves: 4   Portion Size: 1 - 2 ½ ounce Turkey Cutlet

Ingredients:

2 Tbsp	Lemon Juice
2 Tbsp	Water
½ tsp	Ground Tarragon
1 tsp	Minced Garlic
¼ tsp	Salt
¼ tsp	Black Pepper
1 Tbsp	Olive Oil
12 ounces	Turkey Cutlets

Instructions:

In a small bowl, whisk together the sauce ingredients of fresh lemon juice, water, tarragon, garlic, salt and pepper. Set aside.

Lightly spray a large skillet with cooking spray. Heat the oil over high heat, swirling to coat the bottom cook the turkey in a single layer for 2 minutes. Turn over and cook for 3 minutes, or until no longer pink in the center. Transfer to a serving plate. Set aside.

Pour the sauce into the skillet. Cook for 15 to 20 seconds, or until the mixture reduces to about 2 tablespoons, stirring constantly with a flat spatula. Drizzle over the turkey.

Nutritional information per serving:

Calories: 125.2, Protein: 20.7 g, Carbohydrate: .9 g, Dietary Fiber: .1 g, Total Fat: 3.8 g, Saturated Fat: .6 g, Cholesterol: 56.1 mg, Phosphorus: 169.3 mg, Potassium: 253 mg, Sodium: 191.7 mg

CHICKEN MARSALA

Serves: 4   Portion Size: 2 ½ Ounce Chicken Breast, plus Sauce

Ingredients:

10 ounces	Chicken Breast
4 cups	Mushroom Slices
1 tsp	Minced Garlic
1 Tbsp	All Purpose Flour
2 ounces	Marsala Wine
14 ounces	Low Sodium Chicken Stock (pg. 95)
¼ tsp	Salt
¼ tsp	Black Pepper

Instructions:

Coat a large nonstick skillet with cooking spray. Over medium-high heat, sauté chicken breasts for 6 minutes on each side. Remove from pan and set aside. Spray pan again with cooking spray, and reduce heat to medium. Add mushrooms and garlic and sauté until all the liquid is evaporated. Add flour, stirring well to coat the mushrooms. Cook for one more minute. Add wine, stirring well to incorporate the flour. Add chicken stock and turn heat to high. Let simmer for 5 minutes. Add salt and pepper. Serve sauce over chicken breasts.

Nutritional information per serving:

Calories: 151.3, Protein: 19.7 g, Carbohydrate: 8.7 g, Dietary Fiber: .8 g, Total Fat: 2.7 g, Saturated Fat: .6 g, Cholesterol: 45.4 mg, Phosphorus: 245.6 mg, Potassium: 592.4 mg, Sodium: 262.4 mg

CHICKEN PENNE WITH TOMATO SAUCE

Serves: 6   Portion Size: 7/8 Cup

Ingredients:

1 tsp	Ground Fennel
1 tsp	Ground Basil
½ tsp	Ground Coriander
¼ tsp	Black Pepper
12 ounces	Chicken Breast Tenders
1 Tbsp	Olive Oil
4 tsp	Minced Garlic
8 ounces	White Wine
8 ounces	Penne, Uncooked
½ ounce	Shredded Parmesan Cheese
2 Tbsp	Chopped Basil
3 cups	Low Sodium Canned Tomatoes

Instructions:

Combine ground fennel, dried basil, ground coriander and black pepper in a small bowl; rub over chicken. Cut chicken into 1 inch cubes.

Heat oil in a large nonstick skillet over medium-high heat. Add chicken; cook 4 minutes, turning once. Remove from heat; set aside.

Reduce heat to medium. Add garlic; sauté 30 seconds or until garlic is soft. Add tomatoes and wine, scraping pan to loosen browned bits. Bring to a boil. Reduce heat, and simmer 15 minutes. Add chicken, and simmer 5 minutes.

Cook pasta according to package directions, omitting salt and fat. Drain. Toss pasta with sauce in a large bowl. Sprinkle with cheese and basil.

Nutritional information per serving:

Calories: 376.9, Protein: 15.4 g, Carbohydrate: 43.7 g, Dietary Fiber: 3.4 g, Total Fat: 12.7 g, Saturated Fat: 2.7 g, Cholesterol: 24.9 mg, Phosphorus: 245.1 mg, Potassium: 488.1 mg, Sodium: 312.8 mg

GREEK LEMON CHICKEN AND RICE

Serves: 4   Portion Size: 2 ½ ounce Chicken + ½ cup Rice

Ingredients:

1 tsp	Lemon Juice
2 tsp	Olive Oil
1 Tbsp	Minced Garlic
¼ tsp	Ground Oregano
10 ounces	Skinless Chicken Breast
¼ tsp	Salt
¼ tsp	Black Pepper
1 cup	Brown Rice, Uncooked

Instructions:

In a medium bowl, whisk together lemon juice, olive oil, garlic, and oregano. Add chicken breast to marinade and turn to coat. Marinade chicken in refrigerator for 30 minutes. Cook rice according to package directions, omitting salt and fat. Coat a large nonstick skillet with cooking spray. Remove chicken from marinade and season with salt and pepper. Reserve marinade. Cook chicken over high heat for approximately 5 to 7 minutes on each side. Add reserved marinade to pan and bring to a boil for 1 to 2 minutes. Serve chicken breasts over brown rice.

Nutritional information per serving:

Calories: 278, Protein: 18.8 g, Carbohydrate: 37.5 g, Dietary Fiber: 1.7 g, Total Fat: 5.4 g, Saturated Fat: .9 g, Cholesterol: 45.4 mg, Phosphorus: 278.5 mg, Potassium: 408.9 mg, Sodium: 231.5 mg

LEMON BASIL CHICKEN

Serves: 4   Portion Size: 3 ounce Chicken + 1 Tbsp Aioli

Ingredients:

1 Tbsp	Ground Basil
1/3 cup	Chopped Green Onion
3 Tbsp	Lemon Juice
2 Tbsp	Red Wine Vinegar
¼ tsp	Black Pepper
½ tsp	Lemon Peel
2 Tbsp	Lowfat Mayonnaise
½ Tbsp	Dijon Mustard
1 tsp	Minced Garlic
12 ounces	Skinless Chicken Breast

Instructions:

To prepare chicken, combine , 2 tsp basil, onions, lemon juice, wine vinegar, lemon rind, and black pepper in a large bowl. Add chicken to basil mixture, turning to coat.

Heat a large nonstick skillet over medium-high heat. Coat pan with cooking spray. Add chicken to pan; cook 8 minutes on each side or until done.

While chicken cooks, prepare aioli. Combine 1 tsp basil and lowfat mayonnaise, 1 tablespoon lemon juice, dijon mustard, garlic and olive oil in a small bowl, stirring with a whisk. Serve with chicken.

Nutritional information per serving:

Calories: 131.3, Protein: 18.5 g, Carbohydrate: 3.5 g, Dietary Fiber: .4 g,Total Fat: 4.4 g, Saturated Fat: .8 g Cholesterol: 56.3 mg, Phosphorus: 187.6 mg, Potassium: 371.1 mg, Sodium: 155.4 mg

ROASTED LEMON HERB TURKEY BREAST

Serves: 4   Portion Size: 3 ounce Turkey Breast

Ingredients:

1 Tbsp	Olive Oil
12 ounces	Turkey Breast
1 each	Lemon
½ Tbsp	Dried Parsley
½ tsp	Ground Basil
½ Tbsp	Dijon Mustard
1 tsp	Ground Oregano
½ tsp	Black Pepper
½ tsp	Garlic Powder

Instructions:

Preheat the oven to 325°F. Lightly spray a roasting pan baking rack with cooking spray. Cut the lemons in half. Squeeze about ¼ cup juice into a small bowl. Set aside the lemon halves.

Whisk the parsley, basil, mustard, oil, oregano, pepper, and garlic powder into the lemon juice. Cut the breast in half, lengthwise. Spread the lemon juice mixture in the center of the meat, like a stuffed breast, over as much area as possible. Gently put the turkey halves together. Put the turkey on the rack in the pan. Put the lemon halves in the pan directly under the turkey. Sprinkle the top of the turkey with paprika.

Roast the turkey for 30 to 45 minutes or until the thickest part of the breast registers about 155°F on an instant read thermometer. Remove from oven and lightly cover. Let stand for 15 minutes to continue cooking; the breast should reach at least 165°F for easier slicing. Discard the lemons before slicing turkey.

Nutritional information per serving:

Calories: 135.1, Protein: 20.8 g, Carbohydrate: 2 g, Dietary Fiber: .4 g, Total Fat: 4.4 g Saturated Fat: .7 g, Cholesterol: 56.1 mg,Phosphorus: 172.1 mg Potassium: 269.4 mg, Sodium: 59.1 mg

SALSA TURKEY MEATLOAF

Serves: 6   Portion Size: 1/6 of Recipe

Ingredients:

1 lb	Ground Turkey
1 each	Whole Egg
½ cup	Bread Crumbs
½ cup	Chopped Onions
1 tsp	Minced Garlic
¾ cup	Thick and Chunky Salsa

Instructions:

Preheat oven to 400°. Coat a 5 x 9" loaf pan with cooking spray. In a large mixing bowl, combine turkey, egg, bread crumbs, onion, garlic, and 1/2 cup salsa. Mix thoroughly. Place turkey mixture in loaf pan and spread evenly. Top with remaining 1/4 cup salsa. Bake for 50 to 60 minutes. Cut loaf into 6 equal slices.

Nutritional information per serving:

Calories: 176, Protein: 15.8 g, Carbohydrate: 10.1 g, Dietary Fiber: 1.6 g, Total Fat: 7.6 g, Saturated Fat: 2.1 g, Cholesterol: 95.1 mg, Phosphorus: 156.1 mg, Potassium: 231.8 mg, Sodium: 463.1 mg

Salmon and Couscous Bake

Blackened Cumin and Cayenne Tilapia

Crispy Cod

Fish Tacos with Lime Cream Sauce

Halibut with Coconut Curry Sauce

Herbed Filet of Sole

Roasted Shrimp and Broccoli

Seafood Risotto

Snapper with Mango Salsa

Spanish Style Halibut

SALMON AND COUSCOUS BAKE

SALMON AND COUSCOUS BAKE

Serves: 5   *Portion Size:*   *2 ½ ounce Salmon + ½ cup Couscous*

Ingredients:

12 ounces	Salmon
1 cup	Couscous, Unprepared
1 Tbsp	Pine Nuts
1 ½ cups	Water
1 Tbsp	Olive Oil
1 Tbsp	Lemon Juice
1 tsp	Dried Dill Weed
½ cup	Sliced Zucchini
1 ½ cups	Sliced Yellow Squash

Instructions:

Heat oven to 350°F. Spray square baking dish, 8 x 8 x 2 inches, with cooking spray. Cut fish into five serving pieces. Stir couscous, pine nuts, hot water, oil, lemon juice, ½ teaspoon dill weed, zucchini and yellow squash in baking dish. Place fish on couscous mixture. Sprinkle fish with ¼ teaspoon dill weed. Cover and bake 20 to 25 minutes or until liquid is absorbed and fish flakes easily with fork.

Nutritional information per serving:

Calories: 315.3, Protein: 19.1 g, Carbohydrate: 28.8 g, Dietary Fiber: 2.3 g, Total Fat: 13.3 g, Saturated Fat: 2.6 g, Cholesterol: 37.4 mg, Calcium: 27.6 mg, Phosphorus: 250.3 mg, Potassium: 354.7 mg, Sodium: 48.5 mg

BLACKENED CUMIN AND CAYENNE TILAPIA

Serves: 4   Portion Size: 3 ounce Fillet

Ingredients:

1 Tbsp	Olive Oil
12 ounces	Tilapia
2 tsp	Ground Cumin
½ tsp	Salt
½ tsp	Garlic Powder
½ tsp	Cayenne Pepper
¼ tsp	Black Pepper

Instructions:

Preheat broiler.

Rub oil evenly over fish. Combine cumin, salt, garlic powder, cayenne pepper and black pepper; sprinkle over fish. Arrange fish on a broiler pan coated with cooking spray; broil 5 minutes or until fish flakes easily when tested with a fork or desired degree of doneness.

Nutritional information per serving:

Calories: 117.7, Protein: 17.4 g, Carbohydrate: .9 g, Dietary Fiber: .2 g, Total Fat: 5.1 g, Saturated Fat: 1.1 g, Cholesterol: 42.5 mg, Phosphorus: 152.3 mg, Potassium: 286.4 mg, Sodium: 337.1 mg

CRISPY COD

Serves: 4 Portion Size: 3 ounce Filet

Ingredients:

1 ½ cups	Corn Flakes
1 tsp	Minced Garlic
1 tsp	Onion Powder
1 each	Whole Egg
2 each	Egg White
1 tsp	Tabasco Sauce
1/8 cup	All Purpose Flour
12 ounces	Atlantic Cod

Instructions:

Preheat oven to 350°. Coat a shallow baking pan with cooking spray. In a medium bowl, crush corn flakes into crumbs, and combine cornflake crumbs, garlic and onion. In a separate bowl, lightly beat egg and egg whites. Add hot pepper sauce and mix well. Place flour in a separate bowl. Dip each cod fillet in flour, then egg mixture, then cornflake mixture, coating well. Place fillets in baking pan. Spray fillets lightly with cooking spray and bake 18 to 20 minutes.

Nutritional information per serving:

Calories: 146.8, Protein: 19.7 g, Carbohydrate: 12.1 g, Dietary Fiber: .5 g, Total Fat: 1.94 g, Saturated Fat: .5 g, Cholesterol: 89.4 mg, Phosphorus: 210.9 mg, Potassium: 417.8 mg, Sodium: 380.4 mg

FISH TACOS WITH LIME CREAM SAUCE

Serves: 4   Portion Size: 2 Tacos (1 ounce fish per Taco)

Ingredients:

¼ cup	Chopped Green Onions
¼ cup	Chopped Cilantro
3 Tbsp	Fat Free Mayonnaise
3 Tbsp	Reduced Fat Sour Cream
1 each	Lime
1 tsp	Minced Garlic
1 tsp	Ground Cumin
1 tsp	Ground Coriander
½ tsp	Paprika
¼ tsp	Red Pepper Flakes
1/8 tsp	Garlic Powder
10 ounces	Snapper
8 each	Corn Tortillas
2 cups	Shredded Green Cabbage

Instructions:

To prepare lime cream sauce, grate lime rind and squeeze lime juice into bowl. Combine the green onions, cilantro, mayonnaise, sour cream, lime rind, lime juice, and garlic clove in a small bowl; set aside.

To prepare tacos, combine cumin, coriander, paprika, red pepper, and garlic powder in a small bowl; sprinkle spice mixture evenly over both sides of fish. Place fish on a baking sheet coated with cooking spray. Bake at 425° for 9 minutes or until fish flakes easily when tested with a fork or until desired degree of doneness. Place fish in a bowl; break into pieces with a fork. Heat tortillas according to package directions. Divide fish evenly among tortillas; top each with ¼ cup cabbage and 1 tablespoon lime cream sauce.

Nutritional information per serving:

Calories: 225.1, Protein: 18.8 g, Carbohydrate: 29.3 g, Dietary Fiber: 5.1 g, Total Fat: 4.3 g, Saturated Fat: 1.4 g, Cholesterol: 33.1 mg, Phosphorus: 326.5 mg, Potassium: 541.6 mg, Sodium: 177.8 mg

HALIBUT WITH COCONUT CURRY SAUCE

Serves: 4   Portion Size: 4 ounce Filet + ¼ cup Sauce

Ingredients:

2 tsp	Olive Oil
16 ounces	Halibut
1 cup	Chopped Onions
½ cup	Chopped Green Onions
1 Tbsp	Peeled and Sliced Ginger Root
½ cup	Coconut Milk
1 tsp	Sugar
½ Tbsp	Curry Powder
½ tsp	Dried Coriander Leaf
1 Tbsp	Ground Basil
1 ounce	Lime Juice

Instructions:

Heat 1 teaspoon oil in a large nonstick skillet over medium-high heat. Add fish to pan; cook 5 minutes on each side or until fish flakes easily when tested with a fork or until desired degree of doneness. Remove fish from pan; keep warm.

Add remaining 1 teaspoon oil to pan. Add onion, green onions, and ginger; sauté 2 minutes. Stir in coconut milk and sugar, curry, and coriander. Bring to a boil; cook 1 minute. Remove from heat. Stir in basil and juice.

Nutritional information per serving:

Calories: 232.8, Protein: 25.2 g, Carbohydrate: 8.4 g, Dietary Fiber: 1.7 g, Total Fat: 11.1 g, Saturated Fat: 6.1 g, Cholesterol: 36.3 mg, Phosphorus: 305 mg, Potassium: 731.5 mg, Sodium: 70.9 mg

HERBED FILET OF SOLE

Serves: 4   *Portion Size:*   *3 ounce Fish*

Ingredients:

2 Tbsp	Margarine
¼ cup	Lemon Juice
2 tsp	Parsley
2 tsp	Chopped Chives
½ tsp	Ground Tarragon
¼ tsp	Dry Mustard
12 ounces	Sole

Instructions:

Preheat the broiler. Spread the margarine over the bottom of the 13 x 9 x 2 broiler proof baking dish. Set aside.

In a small bowl, stir together the remaining ingredients except the fish. Put the fish in a single layer in the baking dish. Pour half the lemon juice mixture over the fish. Set the remaining mixture aside.

Broil the fish about 4 inches from the heat for about 4 minutes with the oven door partially open to keep the fish from overcooking. Pour the remaining lemon juice mixture over the fish. Broil for 4 to 6 minutes or until the fish flakes easily when tested with a fork.

Nutritional information per serving:

Calories: 126.7, Protein: 16.3 g, Carbohydrate: 1.3 g, Dietary Fiber: .1 g, Total Fat: 6 g, Saturated Fat: 1.2 g, Cholesterol: 40.8 mg, Phosphorus: 161.6 mg, Potassium: 341 mg, Sodium: 122.4 mg

ROASTED SHRIMP AND BROCCOLI

Serves: 4   Portion Size: 1 cup Broccoli + About 6 Shrimp

Ingredients:

5 cups	Chopped Broccoli Florets
½ each	Lemon
½ tsp	Black Pepper
16 ounces	Raw Peeled and Deveined Shrimp
2 Tbsp	Olive Oil
¼ tsp	Red Pepper

Instructions:

Preheat oven to 425°.

Cook broccoli in boiling water 1 minute. Drain and plunge into ice water; drain.

Peel rind off lemon. Place 1 tsp lemon rind into a medium bowl and squeeze juice of lemon into bowl with pepper. Add shrimp; toss to combine. Arrange broccoli and shrimp in a single layer on a jelly-roll pan coated with cooking spray. Bake at 425° for 8 minutes or until shrimp are done.

Combine oil, remaining 1 ½ teaspoons rind, remaining ¼ teaspoon black pepper, and crushed red pepper in a large bowl. Add broccoli; toss to combine.

Nutritional information per serving:

Calories: 201.3, Protein: 19.1 g, Carbohydrate: 9.9 g, Dietary Fiber: 3.6 g, Total Fat: 10.5 g, Saturated Fat: 1.605 g, Cholesterol: 117.1 mg, Phosphorus: 236 mg, Potassium: 528 mg, Sodium: 302.3 mg

SEAFOOD RISOTTO

Serves: 9   Portion Size: 1 Cup

Ingredients:

1 Tbsp	Chopped Onions
2 ½ cups	White Rice (not instant), Dry
28 ounces	Low Sodium Chicken Stock (Pg 95
3 ½ cups	Water
2 tsp	Olive Oil
16 ounces	Scallops
16 ounces	Peeled and Deveined Shrimp
4 ounces	White Wine
½ tsp	Salt
¼ tsp	Black Pepper
¼ cup	Grated Reduced Fat Parmesan Cheese

Instructions:

To make risotto: Coat a large soup pot generously with cooking spray. Over medium to high heat, sauté onions for 3 to 4 minutes or until they turn clear. Stir in rice, and sauté for one more minute. Stir in chicken stock and water and bring to a boil. Reduce heat to a simmer and stir constantly with a large wooden spoon for 20 minutes. Cover and remove from heat.

Add oil to a large nonstick skillet over medium to high heat. Add scallops and shrimp and sauté for 2 minutes. Add wine and cook until wine is reduced by half. Fold seafood, salt, pepper and cheese gently into risotto rice mixture.

Nutritional information per serving:

Calories: 333.7, Protein: 25.3 g, Carbohydrate: 45 g, Dietary Fiber: 1.1 g, Total Fat: 3.8 g, Saturated Fat: 1 g, Cholesterol: 95.7 mg, Phosphorus: 344.2 mg, Potassium: 444.6 mg, Sodium: 358.9 mg

SNAPPER WITH MANGO SALSA

Serves: 4   *Portion Size:*   *3 ounce Fish + 1/3 cup Salsa*

Ingredients:

1 cup	Peeled Mango
½ cup	Sliced Red Onion
2 tsp	Olive Oil
¼ cup	Cubed, Peeled Avocado
2 Tbsp	Fresh Peppermint, Chopped
½ tsp	Lemon Juice
½ tsp	Salt
¼ tsp	Black Pepper
12 ounces	Snapper

Instructions:

Prepare grill to medium-high heat.

Brush mango and onion with 1 teaspoon oil. Place mango and onion on grill rack coated with cooking spray; cover and grill 3 minutes on each side or until tender. Chop onion and mango. Combine onion, mango, avocado, mint, juice, 1/4 teaspoon salt, and 1/8 teaspoon pepper in a medium bowl.

Brush fish with remaining 1 teaspoon oil; sprinkle with 1/4 teaspoon salt and 1/8 teaspoon pepper. Place fish on grill rack; grill 4 minutes on each side or until fish flakes easily when tested with a fork or until desired degree of doneness. Serve with mango mixture. Garnish with mint sprigs, if desired.

Nutritional information per serving:

Calories: 154.2, Protein: 18.1 g, Carbohydrate: 9.6 g, Dietary Fiber: 1.7 g, Total Fat: 4.9 g, Saturated Fat: .8 g, Cholesterol: 31.5 mg, Phosphorus: 183.1 mg, Potassium: 495.6 mg, Sodium: 348.3 mg

SPANISH-STYLE HALIBUT

Serves:	4	Portion Size:	3 ounce Filet + ½ Cup Spinach

Ingredients:

1 slice	Low Sodium Bacon, Uncooked
¼ tsp	Salt
¼ tsp	Paprika
¼ tsp	Black Pepper
12 ounces	Halibut
2 tsp	Minced Garlic
6 ounces	Spinach

Instructions:

Cook the bacon in a large nonstick skillet over medium heat until crisp. Remove bacon from pan, and crumble. Set aside.

Combine ½ teaspoon salt, paprika, and ¼ teaspoon black pepper in a small bowl. Sprinkle spice mixture evenly over fish. Add fish to drippings in pan, and cook for 3 minutes on each side or until fish flakes easily when tested with a fork or until desired degree of doneness. Remove fish from pan, and keep warm.

Add 2 teaspoons garlic to pan, and cook for 1 minute, stirring frequently. Stir in bacon. Add spinach to pan and cook for 1 minute or until the spinach begins to wilt. Serve with fish.

Nutritional information per serving:

Calories: 132.1, Protein: 19.7 g, Carbohydrate: 2.2 g, Dietary Fiber: 1 g, Total Fat: 4.6 g, Saturated Fat: 1.1 g, Cholesterol: 31.1 mg, Phosphorus: 223.1 mg, Potassium: 642.2 mg, Sodium: 272.4 mg

VEGETARIAN ENTREES

Baked Ziti with Veggies

Cheesy Asparagus Soufflé

Curried Eggplant Couscous

Garlic Pasta with Chickpeas

Pumpkin Pasta

Veggie Pitas

BAKED ZITI WITH VEGGIES

Serves: 4   Portion Size: 1 ½ cups

Ingredients:

1 Tbsp	Olive Oil
4 ounces	Ziti, Uncooked
2 cups	Sliced Yellow Summer Squash
1 cup	Chopped Zucchini
½ cup	Chopped Onions
2 cups	Sliced Tomato
2 tsp	Minced Garlic
1 cup	Shredded Mozzarella Cheese
1 Tbsp	Basil
1 tsp	Oregano
¼ tsp	Red Pepper
¼ cup	Low Fat Ricotta
1 each	Whole Egg

Instructions:

Cook pasta according to package directions, omitting salt and fat; drain.

Preheat oven to 400°.

Heat a large skillet over medium-high heat. Add oil to pan. Add squash, zucchini, and onion; sauté 5 minutes. Add tomato and garlic; sauté 3 minutes. Remove from heat; stir in pasta, ½ cup mozzarella, herbs, and pepper.

Combine ricotta and egg. Stir into pasta mixture. Spoon into an 8-inch square glass or ceramic baking dish coated with cooking spray; sprinkle with remaining mozzarella. Bake at 400° for 15 minutes or until bubbly and browned.

Nutritional information per serving:

Calories: 345, Protein: 17.6 g, Carbohydrate: 35.8 g, Dietary Fiber: 4.4 g, Total Fat: 15.2 g, Saturated Fat: 5.2 g, Cholesterol: 72.9 mg, Phosphorus: 314.7 mg, Potassium: 620.5 mg, Sodium: 358.4 mg

CHEESY ASPARAGUS SOUFFLE

Serves: 6   Portion Size: 1/6 of Souffle

Ingredients:

1 Tbsp	Olive Oil
¼ cup	Chopped Onions
½ cup	Sliced Yellow Summer Squash
1 pound	Asparagus
½ cup	Roasted Red Peppers
2 Tbsp	Green Onions, Tops Only
6 each	Whole Eggs
¼ tsp	Black Pepper
¼ tsp	Ground Nutmeg
1 cup	Shredded Swiss Cheese
¼ cup	Grated Reduced Fat Parmesan Cheese

Instructions:

Preheat oven to 400°. Slice the yellow squash into ¼ inch thick circles, then cut in half. Trim asparagus and cut into 1 inch pieces. Cut roasted red peppers into thin strips, and chop the tops of the green onions up.

In a large skillet over medium heat, put the oil, onion, yellow squash, and asparagus; cook, stirring frequently, until fork tender but slightly crisp. Remove skillet from the stove, add the roasted red peppers and green onion tops; stir, then put in a bowl and set aside to let cool.

In a large bowl, put the eggs, pepper and nutmeg and whisk together; add the cheese, tossing to combine. Add the cooled squash and asparagus and stir together. Prepare a loaf pan by spraying with cooking spray, then cut parchment paper to fit; line the bottom of the loaf pan with it and spray the parchment paper surface with more cooking spray.

Pour the mixture into the prepared loaf pan, cut another piece of parchment paper to fit the top, spray the parchment paper with cooking spray, and lay over the top of the mixture. Place the loaf pan in a larger baking dish on the center rack in the oven, then pour hot tap water into the bottom dish so it comes halfway up the loaf pan. Bake in a preheated oven for about an hour or a little more until the middle bounces back when touched. Test with a toothpick stuck in the middle; if it comes out dry, the soufflé is done. Remove and let cool at room temperature for 10 minutes. [continued on next page]

Loosen the edges by running a thin knife around the edges, tip over and slowly slide out of loaf pan. Remove parchment paper pieces. Slice and serve warm.

Nutritional information per serving:

Calories: 193.5, Protein: 13.9 g, Carbohydrate: 5.9 g, Dietary Fiber: 2.0 g, Total Fat: 13.3 g, Saturated Fat: 5.6 g, Cholesterol: 231.7 mg, Phosphorus: 275.9 mg, Potassium: 254.8 mg, Sodium: 200.4 mg

CURRIED EGGPLANT COUSCOUS

Serves: 5   Portion Size: 1 cup

Ingredients:

2 cups	Low Sodium Chicken Stock (pg. 95)
1 cup	Dry Couscous
½ tsp	Salt
¼ tsp	Black Pepper
2 Tbsp	All Purpose Flour
1 Tbsp	Curry Powder
4 cups	Cubed Eggplant
2 tsp	Olive Oil
1 cup	Grated Carrots
½ cup	Golden Raisins

Instructions:

In a medium saucepan, bring 1 ¼ cups chicken stock to a boil; reserve remaining ¾ cup. Add 1 cup uncooked couscous. Cover and remove from heat. Let stand for 5 minutes and fluff with fork. In a large mixing bowl, combine salt, pepper, flour, and curry powder. Add eggplant and toss to coat. Add oil to a large nonstick skillet over medium to high heat. Add eggplant and stir fry for 5 minutes. Add remaining ¾ cup chicken stock and stir well to incorporate the flour. Add carrots and raisins and cook one more minute. Stir in couscous and mix well.

Nutritional information per serving:

Calories: 251.7, Protein: 8.2 g, Carbohydrate: 50.1 g, Dietary Fiber: 5.7 g, Total Fat: 3.1 g, Saturated Fat: .5 g, Cholesterol: 0 mg, Phosphorus: 138.6 mg, Potassium: 508.5 mg, Sodium: 284.1 mg

GARLIC PASTA WITH CHICKPEAS

Serves: 4   Portion Size: 1 cup Pasta + 2 ¼ tsp Cheese

Ingredients:

2 tsp	Olive Oil
4 tsp	Minced Garlic
¼ tsp	Red Pepper Flakes
1 cup	Chickpeas, Drained and Rinsed
14 ounces	Low Sodium Chicken Stock (pg. 95)
1 ¼ cups	Cooked Pasta Shells
1 tsp	Dried Parsley Flakes
1 Tbsp	Lemon Juice
3 Tbsp	Shredded Parmesan

Instructions:

Heat oil in a medium saucepan over medium heat. Add 2 teaspoons crushed garlic; sauté 1 minute. Add salt, pepper, chickpeas, and chicken stock; bring to a boil. Cover, reduce heat, and simmer 15 minutes.

While garlic mixture simmers, cook pasta in boiling water 9 minutes, omitting salt and fat; drain well.

Place chickpea mixture in a food processor, and process until smooth. Combine chickpea mixture, pasta, 2 teaspoons minced garlic, fresh parsley, and lemon juice; toss well. Sprinkle with cheese. Serve immediately.

Nutritional information per serving:

Calories: 305.9, Protein: 13.2 g, Carbohydrate: 51 g, Dietary Fiber: 5 g, Total Fat: 5.6 g, Saturated Fat: 1.4 g, Cholesterol: 2.7 mg, Phosphorus: 185.6 mg, Potassium: 205.9 mg, Sodium: 533 mg

PUMPKIN PASTA

Serves: 10   *Portion Size:*   *1 cup*

Ingredients:

16 ounces	Uncooked Farfalle Pasta
1 tsp	Olive Oil
7 ounces	Light Cream Cheese, Cubed
¼ cup	Grated Reduced Fat Parmesan Cheese
¼ cup	Skim Milk
15 ounces	Canned Pumpkin
½ tsp	Cayenne Pepper Spice
1 tsp	Salt
¼ tsp	Black Pepper
¼ tsp	Ground Sage
¼ tsp	Ground Nutmeg

Instructions:

Cook pasta according to package directions, omitting salt. Drain. Dice cream cheese. In a large saucepan, heat olive oil, cream cheese, parmesan cheese and milk over low heat until cream cheese is melted, stirring frequently. Add remaining ingredients and cook until thoroughly heated. Add cooked pasta to pan and toss gently to coat.

Nutritional information per serving:

Calories: 242, Protein: 9.2 g, Carbohydrate: 39.2 g, Dietary Fiber: 2.7 g, Total Fat: 5.2 g, Saturated Fat: 2.8 g, Cholesterol: 13.4 mg, Phosphorus: 154.5 mg, Potassium: 237.5 mg, Sodium: 337 mg

VEGGIE PITAS

Serves: 4   *Portion Size:*   *1 Pita*

Ingredients:

4 each	Large Whole Wheat Pita Bread
2 Tbsp	Light Mayonnaise
1 tsp	Minced Garlic
¾ cup	Hummus
¼ cup	Sunflower Kernels
4 each	Romaine Leaves
1 cup	Sliced Red Onions
1 ½ cup	Sliced Cucumber

Instructions:

Slice 1 side of each pita to open a pocket, but do not cut all the way through. Set aside. In a small bowl, whisk together mayonnaise and garlic. Spread 1 tablespoon of mayonnaise in each pita. Spread ¼ cup of hummus on each pita, and sprinkle 2 teaspoons of sunflower seeds on top. Layer leaf lettuce, onion slices, and cucumber slices on top of hummus.

Nutritional information per serving:

Calories: 405.5, Protein: 16.6, Carbohydrate: 56.6 g, Dietary Fiber: 9.8 g, Total Fat: 14.4 g, Saturated Fat: 2.3 g, Cholesterol: 8.206 mg, Phosphorus: 285 mg, Potassium: 394 mg, Sodium: 449.8 mg

SALADS

Spring Greens with Strawberries and Blue Cheese

Bacon and Shrimp Salad

Chicken Pasta Salad with Mozzarella

Chinese Chicken Salad

Grilled Peaches À La Rosemary Salad

Sweet and Sour Summer Squash Slaw

SPRING GREENS WITH STRAWBERRIES AND BLUE CHEESE

SPRING GREENS WITH STRAWBERRIES AND BLUE CHEESE

Serves: 4   Portion Size: ¼ of Recipe

Ingredients:

6 cups	Chopped Iceburg Lettuce
2 cups	Whole Strawberries
¼ cup	Sliced Red Onions
1/3 cup	Cranberry Juice
2 Tbsp	Honey
1 ½ Tbsp	Balsamic Vinegar
¼ tsp	Lemon Peel
¼ tsp	Ground Cumin
¼ tsp	Ground Cinnamon
¼ cup	Crumbled Blue Cheese

Instructions:

Clean strawberries, and quarter them.

In a shallow serving dish, arrange the lettuce, strawberries, and onion.

In a small bowl, whisk together the cranberry juice, honey, balsamic vinegar, lemon peel, cumin and cinnamon. Pour over the salad. Sprinkle the blue cheese (1 tablespoon per salad) on the salad. Serve immediately for the best taste with 2 tablespoons dressing per salad.

Nutritional information per serving:

Calories: 115, Protein: 3.2 g, Carbohydrate: 21.3 g, Dietary Fiber: 2.7 g, Total Fat: 2.8 g, Saturated Fat: 1.6 g, Cholesterol: 6.328 mg, Phosphorus: 73.5 mg, Potassium: 290 mg, Sodium: 129.4 mg

BACON AND SHRIMP SALAD

Serves: 4   Portion Size: 2 ¼ cups Salad Mix

Ingredients:

3 slices	Low Sodium Bacon
12 ounces	Shrimp
5 cups	Arugula
½ cup	Chopped Red Tomato
2 Tbsp	Lowfat Plain Yogurt
2 Tbsp	Balsamic Vinegar
2 Tbsp	Olive Oil
¼ tsp	Black Pepper

Instructions:

Cook bacon in a large nonstick skillet over medium heat until crisp. Remove bacon from the pan, reserving 1 teaspoon drippings in pan. Crumble bacon, and set aside. Add shrimp to drippings in the pan; sauté 5 minutes or until done. Using a slotted spoon, transfer shrimp to a large bowl. Add arugula leaves and chopped tomatoes to shrimp; toss gently.

Dressing - Combine yogurt, vinegar, oil, and pepper in a small bowl, stirring well with a whisk. Drizzle vinegar mixture over shrimp mixture; toss gently to combine. Place 2 ¼ cups salad mixture on each of 4 plates; divide crumbled bacon evenly among salads.

Nutritional information per serving:

Calories: 254.2, Protein: 20.7 g, Carbohydrate: 5.5 g, Dietary Fiber: .9 g, Total Fat: 16.3 g, Saturated Fat: 3.8 g, Cholesterol: 141.3 mg, Phosphorus: 242.9 mg, Potassium: 420.2 mg, Sodium: 283.9 mg

CHICKEN PASTA SALAD WITH MOZZARELLA

Serves: 8   Portion Size: 1 Cup

Ingredients:

5 Tbsp	Balsamic Vinegar
2 Tbsp	Olive Oil
½ Tbsp	Dijon Mustard
8 ounces	Penne Pasta, Uncooked
12 ounces	Skinless Chicken Breast
2 cups	Sliced Tomato
¼ cup	Parsley
6 ounces	Part Skim Mozzarella, Cubed

Instructions:

In a small bowl, whisk together, balsamic vinegar, olive oil, and dijon mustard. Cook pasta according to package directions, omitting salt. Drain pasta and run under cold water until pasta is cooled. Fully cook chicken and cut into cubes. Cut mozzarella cheese into cubes as well. In a large bowl, toss cooled pasta with remaining salad ingredients. Drizzle dressing over salad and toss well to coat.

Nutritional information per serving:

Calories: 258.7, Protein: 18.4 g, Carbohydrate: 25.6 g, Dietary Fiber: 1.5 g, Total Fat: 8.7 g, Saturated Fat: 3 g, Cholesterol: 40.8 mg, Phosphorus: 255.4 mg, Potassium: 366.8 mg, Sodium: 195 mg

CHINESE CHICKEN SALAD

Serves: 4   Portion Size: ¼ of Mixture

Ingredients:

1 Tbsp	Sesame Oil
¼ cup	Peeled and Sliced Ginger Root
2 Tbsp	Minced Garlic
½ cup	Chopped Green Onions
1 Tbsp	Cornstarch
2 Tbsp	Low Sodium Soy Sauce
½ cup	Low Sodium Chicken Stock, (pg. 95)
3 Tbsp	Rice Vinegar
¼ cup	Low Sodium Ketchup
1 Tbsp	Black Pepper
¼ cup	Lime Juice
1 tsp	Chili Powder
8 ounces	Chicken Breast
4 cups	Shredded Red Cabbage
4 ounces	Snow Pea Pods
½ cup	Chopped Cilantro
2 Tbsp	Sesame Seeds

Instructions:

Heat a large nonstick sauté pan over high heat. When the pan is hot, add the sesame oil. Add the ginger, garlic, and onions, and sauté, stirring often, about 2 minutes. Meanwhile, place the cornstarch in a medium bowl. Add the soy sauce, chicken stock, vinegar, and ketchup and whisk to blend. Whisk the cornstarch mixture into the sauté pan and bring sauce to a simmer. Reduce the heat to medium and simmer, whisking constantly, until the sauce has thickened, about 2 minutes. Cook chicken, then shred into small pieces.

In a large bowl, whisk together the sauce you just made, lime juice and chili powder. Add the shredded chicken, red cabbage, snow peas, cilantro, and sesame seeds. Toss the salad to combine. Chill in the refrigerator until serving time, up to 6 hours.

Nutritional information per serving:

Calories: 215.6, Protein: 17.7 g, Carbohydrate: 20.7 g, Dietary Fiber: 4.1 g, Total Fat: 7.8 g, Saturated Fat: 1.3 g, Cholesterol: 35.3 mg, Phosphorus: 203.4 mg, Potassium: 587.2 mg, Sodium: 450.7 mg

GRILLED PEACHES A LA ROSEMARY SALAD

Serves: 4   Portion Size: ¼ of Salad

Ingredients:

2 each	Medium Peaches
5 Tbsp	Olive Oil
1 tsp	Dried Rosemary
2 cups	Arugula
1 cup	Mozzarella Cheese
4 Tbsp	Balsamic Vinegar
2 cups	Chopped Iceburg Lettuce

Instructions:

Take your ripe but still firm peaches, and wash and cut them in half removing the pits. Prepare a grilling pan by spraying with nonstick grilling oil, then set grill to medium heat. Put peach halves in bowl with 1 Tbsp olive oil, and rosemary, and toss to coat. When grill is preheated, put the peaches on, cut side down and grill for 4 to 5 minutes, until charred lightly, then flip and grill 3 to 4 more minutes until softened slightly and charred. Remove and set aside to cool slightly.

Prepare individual salads by arranging iceberg lettuce between four salad plates, then top each plate with ½ cup arugula. Place one grilled peach half on top of the arugula, and add ¼ cup mozzarella for each salad and place on top. Drizzle with a little balsamic vinegar and olive oil (1 tablespoon each), sprinkle with a dash of salt and freshly ground black pepper to taste. Serve immediately.

Nutritional information per serving:

Calories: 285.3, Protein: 8.6 g, Carbohydrate: 12.4 g, Dietary Fiber: 1.7 g, Total Fat: 22.9 g, Saturated Fat: 5.4 g Cholesterol: 15.3 mg, Phosphorus: 177.2 mg, Potassium: 267.4 mg, Sodium: 158.9 mg

SWEET AND SOUR SUMMER SQUASH SLAW

Serves: 4   Portion Size: ¼ of Recipe

Ingredients:

3 each	Small Yellow Summer Squash
3 each	Baby Zucchini
2 stalks	Celery, Chopped
3 each	Green Onions, Chopped
½ each	Red Bell Pepper, Diced
¼ each	Green Bell Pepper, Diced
¼ cup	Sugar
¼ cup	Cider Vinegar
¼ cup	Olive Oil
5 sprigs	Dill Weed, Chopped
1 tsp	Ground Basil
½ tsp	Ground Thyme
½ tsp	Black Pepper

Instructions:

Scrub the squash well, trim off both ends, then take a peeler and start peeling off long curls into a colander. Let drain over the sink for about 20 minutes. This will help the squash sweat off some of the moisture. Dump into a large surface covered with paper towels and use paper towels to blot off liquid, then dump squash curls in large salad bowl. To the salad bowl add the celery onions and red and green bell peppers.

Next add the sugar, apple cider vinegar, olive oil, dill, basil, thyme, black pepper into a bowl and whisk together until well combined. You could also put the ingredients in a jar with a good lid and shake to combine. When dressing is well mixed, immediately drizzle a little over salad, mix, taste and add more dressing as desired tossing to coat after each addition. When this slaw has the right amount dressing, serve immediately or chill until ready to eat.

Nutritional information per serving:

Calories: 205.2, Protein: 2.1 g, Carbohydrate: 19.7 g, Dietary Fiber: 2.7 g, Total Fat: 13.9 g, Saturated Fat: 1.9 g, Cholesterol: 0 mg, Phosphorus: 63.9 mg, Potassium: 240.3 mg, Sodium: 32.1 mg

SOUPS

Low Sodium Chicken Stock

Beef Broth

Vegetable Broth

Ancho Pork and Hominy Stew

Chili Con Carne

Corn and White Bean Soup

Turkey and White Bean Chili

Vegetable and Bean Chili

Vegetarian Stew

*A WORD OF CAUTION ABOUT THE SOUPS. MANY MAY BE CONSIDERED TO BE HIGH POTASSIUM SOUPS. NOT EVERY PERSON WHO HAS STAGE 3 OR 4 KIDNEY DISEASE NEEDS LOW POTASSIUM, AND SO I AM SHOWING A VARIETY OF FOODS. IF YOU NEED LOW POTASSIUM, PAY ATTENTION TO THE NUTRITIONAL INFORMATION AND AVOID THOSE WITH A HIGHER AMOUNT OF POTASSIUM.

LOW SODIUM CHICKEN STOCK

Serves: 12   Portion Size: 1/12 of Recipe

Ingredients:

1 ½ lb	Light Meat from Chicken Broiler or Fryer
1 ½ lb	Dark Meat from Chicken Broiler or Fryer
2-3 lb	Chicken Bones (Optional)
12 cups	Water
1 cup	Chopped Carrots
4 stalks	Celery
4 cloves	Garlic, Whole
1 cup	Chopped Onions
1 each	Whole Bay Leaf
1 tsp	Ground Thyme
½ tsp	Dried Rosemary
½ tsp	Black Pepper
5-6 each	Peppercorns

Instructions:

In a stock pot, stir together all the ingredients. Bring to a boil over high heat. Skim any foam off the top. Reduce the heat and simmer, covered, for 1 to 2 hours if not using the extra bones or 3 to 4 hours with the extra bones. (To prevent cloudiness, don't let the chicken stock return to a boil).

Remove the chicken and reserve for another use. Discard the bones. Strain the chicken stock into an airtight container, discarding the vegetables, peppercorns, and bay leaf. Cover and refrigerate chicken stock for 1 to 2 hours, or until the fat hardens on the surface. Discard the hardened fat before reheating the chicken stock.

Nutritional information per serving:

Calories: 8, Protein: 2 g, Carbohydrate: 0 g, Total Sugars: 0 g, Total Fat: 0 g, Saturated Fat: 0 g, Cholesterol: 0 mg, Phosphorus: 70 mg, Potassium: 75 mg, Sodium: 19 mg

BEEF BROTH

Serves: 12   *Portion Size:*   *1/12 of Recipe*

Ingredients:

4 lb	Beef or Veal Bones, preferably shank or knuckle bones
12 cups	Water
1 cup	Chopped Onion
1 tsp	Crumbled Bay Leaf
10 sprigs	Parsley
5-6 each	Peppercorns
1 tsp	Ground Thyme

Instructions:

Preheat the oven to 400°F. Lightly spray a roasting pan with cooking spray. Put the beef bones, preferably shank or knuckle bones, in the pan. Roast for 25 to 30 minutes, turning once halfway through. Using tongs, transfer the balance to a stock pot.

Add the remaining ingredients to the pot. Bring to a boil over high heat. Skim off any foam that comes to the top. Reduce the heat and simmer, covered, for 4 to 6 hours. To prevent cloudiness, don't let the broth return to a boil. Strain the broth into an airtight container, discarding the solids. Cover and refrigerate the broth for 1 to 2 hours, or until the fat hardens on the surface. Discard the hardened fat before reheating the broth.

Nutritional information per serving:

Calories: 8, Protein: 2 g, Carbohydrate: 0 g, Dietary Fiber: 0 g, Total Fat: 0 g, Saturated Fat: .0 g, Cholesterol: 0 mg, Phosphorus: 70 mg, Potassium: 75 mg, Sodium: 23 mg

VEGETABLE BROTH

Serves: 8   Portion Size: 1/8 of Recipe

Ingredients:

4 cups   Vegetable Trimmings
6 cups   Water
¼ tsp   Black Pepper

Instructions:

For the vegetable trimmings, use low potassium vegetables like asparagus, cabbage, carrots, cauliflower, celery, cucumber, eggplant, mushrooms, onions, peppers, radishes, yellow squash and zucchini. You can use small amounts of high potassium vegetables as well. In a stock pot, stir together all the ingredients. Bring to a boil over high heat. Skim off any foam that comes to the top. Reduce the heat and simmer, covered, for one hour. To prevent cloudiness, don't let the broth return to a boil. Strain the broth into an airtight container, discarding the solids. Cover and refrigerate the broth so the flavors blend.

You can keep a bag in the freezer to hold your vegetable trimmings and collect vegetable peels. That way when it's time to make the vegetable broth, you have plenty to use.

Nutritional information per serving:

Calories: 6, Protein: 1 g, Carbohydrate: 1 g, Dietary Fiber: 0 g, Total Fat: 0 g, Saturated Fat: 0g, Cholesterol: 0 mg, Phosphorus: 15 mg, Potassium: 20 mg, Sodium: 18 mg

ANCHO PORK AND HOMINY STEW

Serves: 6   Portion Size: 1 ¼ cup

Ingredients:

2 Tbsp	Ancho Chile Powder
2 tsp	Ground Oregano
1 ½ tsp	Smoked Paprika
1 tsp	Ground Cumin
12 ounces	Pork Tenderloin
1 Tbsp	Olive Oil
2 cups	Chopped Onions
1 ½ cups	Chopped Green Bell Pepper
1 Tbsp	Minced Garlic
3 cups	Low Sodium Chicken Stock (pg. 95)
2 cups	White Hominy, Drained and Rinsed
1 ½ cups	Diced Canned Tomato, Low Sodium

Instructions:

Combine ancho chile powder, dried oregano, paprika, and cumin in a large bowl; set 1 ½ teaspoons spice mixture aside. Add pork to remaining spice mixture in bowl, tossing well to coat.

Heat 2 teaspoons oil in a large Dutch oven over medium-high heat. Add pork mixture to pan; cook 5 minutes or until browned, stirring occasionally. Remove pork from pan; set aside. Add remaining 1 teaspoon oil to pan. Add onion, bell pepper, and garlic; sauté 5 minutes or until tender, stirring occasionally. Return pork to pan. Add reserved 1 ½ teaspoons spice mixture, broth, hominy, and tomatoes; bring to a boil. Partially cover, reduce heat, and simmer 25 minutes.

Nutritional information per serving:

Calories: 193.8, Protein: 16.6 g, Carbohydrate: 21.1 g, Dietary Fiber: 4.8 g, Total Fat: 6 g, Saturated Fat: 1.3 g, Cholesterol: 27.8 mg, Phosphorus: 265.9 mg, Potassium: 737.9 mg Sodium: 322.7 mg

CHILI CON CARNE

CHILI CON CARNE

Serves: 4   Portion Size: 1 cup

Ingredients:

1 lb	93-95% Lean Ground Beef
1 cup	Low Sodium Stewed Tomatoes
1 Tbsp	Olive Oil
2 Tbsp	Chili Powder
½ cup	Chopped Onions
¼ cup	Chopped Celery
½ cup	Chopped Green Bell Pepper
2 cups	Water

Instructions:

Heat large skillet on medium heat. Add oil, onion, celery and pepper until tender but not brown. Blenderize the stewed tomatoes.

Add ground beef, breaking into small pieces and cook until brown.

Add blenderized tomatoes, chili powder, and water. Mix thoroughly; reduce heat to low.

Simmer covered for several hours.

You can make this up ahead of time and separate into portions to freeze; thaw and reheat when you are ready to eat another serving.

Nutritional information per serving:

Calories: 169.3, Protein: 16.1 g, Carbohydrate: 7.1 g, Dietary Fiber: 1.3 g, Total Fat: 10.3 g, Saturated Fat: 3.5 g, Cholesterol: 49.1 mg, Phosphorus: 175 mg, Potassium: 469.5 mg, Sodium: 102.8 mg

CORN AND WHITE BEAN SOUP

Serves: 6   Portion Size: 1 ½ cups

Ingredients:

1 Tbsp	Olive Oil
1 cup	Chopped Green Onion
4 ounces	Cubed Cooked Low Sodium Ham
3 cups	Frozen Sweet Corn
2 cups	Canned Navy Beans
2 cups	Low Sodium Chicken Stock (pg. 95)
1 cup	Chili Sauce

Instructions:

Heat olive oil in a Dutch oven over medium heat. Add onions and ham, and cook 3 minutes, stirring frequently. Rinse and drain navy beans before putting into soup. Stir in corn and remaining ingredients. Bring to a boil; reduce heat, and simmer 5 minutes or until thoroughly heated.

Nutritional information per serving:

Calories: 256.6, Protein: 16.3 g, Carbohydrate: 36.2 g, Dietary Fiber: 7.3 g, Total Fat: 5.4 g, Saturated Fat: 1.2 g, Cholesterol: 11 mg, Phosphorus: 309.1 mg, Potassium: 440.2 mg, Sodium: 300 mg

TURKEY AND WHITE BEAN CHILI

Serves: 4   Portion Size: 1 cup

Ingredients:

10 ounces	Ground Turkey
½ cup	Chopped Onion
2 tsp	Minced Garlic
1 Tbsp	Olive Oil
1 Tbsp	Chili Powder
1 tsp	Ground Cumin
1 cup	Canned White Cannellini Beans
1 ½ cup	Low Sodium Canned Stewed Tomatoes
2 cups	Low Sodium Chicken Stock (pg. 95)

Instructions:

Heat oil in a large saucepan over medium-high heat. Add onion and cook, stirring occasionally, until softened, about 5 minutes. Add garlic and cook 1 minute more. Add turkey, chili powder, and cumin; cook, stirring often, until turkey is no longer pink inside, about 5 minutes. Rinse and drain beans. Add beans, tomatoes with juice, and chicken stock; bring to a boil. Reduce heat to medium to low, cover, and simmer until flavors blend, about 15 minutes.

Nutritional information per serving:

Calories: 251.2, Protein: 19.6 g, Carbohydrate: 20.9 g, Dietary Fiber: 5.5 g, Total Fat: 10.8 g, Saturated Fat: 2.4 g, Cholesterol: 56 mg, Phosphorus: 240.2 mg, Potassium: 610.3 mg, Sodium: 350 mg

VEGETABLE AND BEAN CHILI

Serves: 8   *Portion Size:*   *1 cup*

Ingredients:

1 Tbsp	Olive Oil
½ cup	Chopped Onions
2 cups	Chopped Carrots
½ cup	Chopped Green Bell Pepper
1 cup	Chopped Zucchini
2 tsp	Minced Garlic
1 tsp	Chili Powder
1 ½ cup	Kidney Beans, Drained and Rinsed
1 ½ cup	Black Beans, Drained and Rinsed
8 ounces	Tomato Sauce, no salt added
4 cups	Low Sodium Chicken Stock (pg. 95)

Instructions:

Heat oil in a large soup pot over medium-high heat. Add onion and carrots, and sauté 5 minutes. Drain and rinse beans prior to use. Add green bell pepper and, zucchini and sauté another 2 minutes. Add garlic and sauté for 30 seconds. Add chili powder, and all remaining ingredients; bring to a boil. Cover, reduce heat, and simmer 30 to 35 minutes or until the vegetables are tender.

Nutritional information per serving:

Calories: 156.3, Protein: 9.3 g, Carbohydrate: 24.8 g, Dietary Fiber: 7 g, Total Fat: 3.1 g, Saturated Fat: .6 g, Cholesterol: 0 mg, Phosphorus: 161.8 mg, Potassium: 651.8 mg, Sodium: 73.4 mg

VEGETARIAN STEW

Serves: 7   *Portion Size:*   *1 cup*

Ingredients:

¼ cup	Low Sodium Chicken Stock (pg. 95)
1 ½ cups	Sliced Zucchini
1 ½ cups	Chopped Carrots
1 cup	Chopped Celery
2 each	Peeled Diced Potato
2 cups	Diced Tomatoes, No Salt Added
1 tsp	Paprika
1 ½ tsp	Ground Cumin
1 tsp	Onion Powder
1 16 oz can	Garbanzo Beans, Rinsed
¼ tsp	Salt
¼ tsp	Black Pepper

Instructions:

In a large soup pot, add chicken stock, zucchini, carrots, celery and potatoes and heat over medium to high temperature. Simmer for 5 to 6 minutes or until vegetables just begin to soften. Add remaining ingredients and bring to a boil. Reduce heat and simmer, covered, for 30 minutes.

Nutritional information per serving:

Calories: 154, Protein: 6.6 g, Carbohydrate: 29.9 g, Dietary Fiber: 6.91 g, Total Fat: 1.7 g, Saturated Fat: .2 g, Cholesterol: 0 mg, Phosphorus: 138.6 mg, Potassium: 703.6 mg, Sodium: 304.6 mg

SIDE DISHES

Pineapple Slaw

Balsamic Green Beans

Barley and Asparagus

Cauliflower Florets with Lemon Mustard Butter

Cucumber and Onion Salad

Coconut Rice

Faux Mashed Potatoes

Fried Rice

Garden Coleslaw with Almonds

Green Bean Salad with Quinoa

Italian Green Beans

Orzo with Herbs

Roasted Garlic Carrots

Roasted Parmesan Zucchini

Sage Sweet Potato Turnip Mash

Savory Grits

Vegetable Paella

PINEAPPLE SLAW

PINEAPPLE SLAW

Serves: 6   Portion Size: ½ cup

Ingredients:

2 Tbsp   Sugar
2 Tbsp   Cider Vinegar
¼ tsp   Black Pepper
½ cup   Light Mayonnaise
8 ounces   Crushed Pineapple
3 cups   Shredded Cabbage

Instructions:

Combine sugar, vinegar, pepper and mayonnaise. Add pineapple with juice. Toss with shredded cabbage. Allow to chill in refrigerator for one hour prior to serving. Divide into six servings.

Nutritional information per serving:

Calories: 113.8, Protein: .8 g, Carbohydrate: 13.9 g, Dietary Fiber: 1.2 g, Total Fat: 6.7 g, Saturated Fat: 1.1 g, Cholesterol: 7 mg, Phosphorus: 18.9 mg, Potassium: 118.4 mg, Sodium: 141.6 mg

BALSAMIC GREEN BEANS

Serves: 6   Portion Size: ½ cup each

Ingredients:

2 Tbsp	Balsamic Vinegar
1 Tbsp	Brown Sugar
1 tsp	Dijon Mustard
1 Tbsp	Olive Oil
½ tsp	Black Pepper
1 ½ lb	Frozen Green Beans

Instructions:

Cook beans until tender and drain. Combine balsamic vinegar, brown sugar, and dijon mustard with olive oil and pepper then toss with beans. Heat in microwave for another 30 seconds to a minute until hot.

Nutritional information per serving:

Calories: 81.2, Protein: 2.1 g, Carbohydrate: 12 g, Dietary Fiber: 3 g, Total Fat: 2.7 g, Saturated Fat: .407 g, Cholesterol: 0 mg, Phosphorus: 37.9 mg, Potassium: 222.3 mg, Sodium: 11.3 mg

BARLEY AND ASPARAGUS

Serves: 10   Portion Size: 1/3 cup

Ingredients:

2 Tbsp	Olive Oil
½ cup	Chopped Onions
½ cup	Chopped Carrots
1 cup	Pearled Barley
3 ½ cups	Low Sodium Chicken Stock (pg. 95)
1 cup	Asparagus
2 Tbsp	Grated Reduced Fat Parmesan Cheese
½ tsp	Dried Marjoram
¼ tsp	Black Pepper

Instructions:

Cut asparagus into 1 inch pieces. Chop onion and carrots. Heat oil in a 12 inch skillet over medium heat. Cook onion and carrot in oil 1 to 2 minutes, stirring occasionally, until crisp-tender. Stir in barley. Cook and stir 1 minute. Using chicken stock from recipe, pour 1 cup of the hot chicken stock over barley mixture. Cook uncovered about 5 minutes, stirring occasionally, until liquid is absorbed. Stir in asparagus. Continue cooking 15 to 20 minutes, adding chicken stock 1 cup at a time and stirring frequently, until barley is tender and liquid is absorbed; remove from heat. Stir in remaining ingredients.

Nutritional information per serving:

Calories: 105.6, Protein: 2.6 g, Carbohydrate: 17.5 g, Dietary Fiber: 3.7 g, Total Fat: 3.1 g, Saturated Fat: .5 g, Cholesterol: .8 mg, Phosphorus: 63.2 mg, Potassium: 118.5 mg, Sodium: 24.7 mg

CAULIFLOWER FLORETS WITH LEMON MUSTARD BUTTER

Serves: 8   Portion Size: ½ cup

Ingredients:

2 Tbsp	Margarine
1 Tbsp	Dijon Mustard
2 tsp	Lemon Peel
¼ cup	Chopped Green Onions
4 cups	Cauliflower

Instructions:

In a small bowl, whisk together the margarine, dijon mustard, lemon peel, and chopped onion. Steam cauliflower florets until tender crisp. In a large saucepan, add cauliflower and margarine mixture over low heat. Toss gently until cauliflower is coated.

Nutritional information per serving:

Calories: 33.3, Protein: 1 g, Carbohydrate: 3.4 g, Dietary Fiber: 1.3 g, Total Fat: 2.1 g, Saturated Fat: .4 g, Cholesterol: 0 mg, Phosphorus: 23.9 mg, Potassium: 162.3 mg, Sodium: 50.2 mg

CUCUMBER AND ONION SALAD

Serves: 5   Portion Size: ½ cup

Ingredients:

½ cup   Nonfat Milk
4 Tbsp   Reduced Fat Sour Cream
1 tsp   Dried Dill Weed
1 tsp   Minced Garlic
1½ Tbsp   Red Wine Vinegar
¼ tsp   Black Pepper
2 tsp   Splenda
2 cups   Sliced Cucumber
1 each   Onion, Sliced

Instructions:

In a medium bowl, whisk together all ingredients except cucumber and onion. Add cucumber and onion and toss to coat well. Serve chilled.

Nutritional information per serving:

Calories: 62.6, Protein: 2.8 g, Carbohydrate: 9.2 g, Dietary Fiber: 1 g, Total Fat: 1.6 g, Saturated Fat: 1 g, Cholesterol: 6.7 mg, Phosphorus: 82.5 mg, Potassium: 244 mg, Sodium: 33.3 mg

COCONUT RICE

Serves: 4   Portion Size: ½ cup

Ingredients:

1 cup	Uncooked Basmati Rice
10 ounces	Water
½ cup	Coconut Milk
¼ tsp	Salt

Instructions:

Combine basmati rice, water, coconut milk and salt in a small saucepan. Bring to a boil. Cover, reduce heat and simmer 16 minutes or until liquid is absorbed.

Nutritional information per serving:

Calories: 224.5, Protein: 3.8 g, Carbohydrate: 37.8 g, Dietary Fiber: .6 g, Total Fat: 6.3 g, Saturated Fat: 5.4 g, Cholesterol: 0 mg, Phosphorus: 80.3 mg, Potassium: 116.1 mg, Sodium: 153.5 mg

FAUX MASHED POTATOES

Serves: 6   Portion Size: 1/6 of Recipe

Ingredients:

1 each	Medium Cauliflower Head
1 Tbsp	Cream Cheese
¼ cup	Grated Reduced Fat Parmesan Cheese
1 tsp	Minced Garlic
1/8 tsp	Black Pepper
1 Tbsp	Unsalted Butter

Instructions:

Clean and wash cauliflower, then cut into even small size pieces.

Bring a big pot of water to a boil, drop cauliflower pieces in and cook for about 5 to 7 minutes or until very tender.

Drain well, then dump onto a surface covered in paper towels to remove any leftover moisture; do not let cool off. Put warm cauliflower in food processor or blender and add the remaining ingredients. Pulse process until blended well and has the consistency of mashed potatoes. Don't over blend: leave some lumps or the mixture will start to get runny.

Nutritional information per serving:

Calories: 61.6, Protein: 2.9 g, Carbohydrate: 5.2 g, Dietary Fiber: 2 g, Total Fat: 3.8 g, Saturated Fat: 2.3 g, Cholesterol: 11.4 mg, Phosphorus: 77.4 mg, Potassium: 304.6 mg, Sodium: 101.2 mg

FRIED RICE

Serves: 6   Portion Size: ¾ cup

Ingredients:

2 Tbsp	Canola Oil
4 each	Whole Eggs
¼ tsp	Black Pepper
1 ¾ cups	Chopped Green Onions
1 tsp	Ground Ginger
2 tsp	Minced Garlic
1 ½ cups	Uncooked Brown Rice
2 Tbsp	Low Sodium Soy Sauce
2 cups	Peas
1 sprig	Cilantro

Instructions:

Cook rice fully and set aside. Heat 2 teaspoons oil in a large nonstick skillet over medium-high heat. Add half of eggs; swirl to coat bottom of pan evenly. Sprinkle with 1/8 teaspoon pepper; cook 3 minutes or until egg is done. Remove egg from pan; thinly slice, and set aside.

Wipe pan clean with a paper towel. Heat remaining 4 teaspoons oil in pan over medium-high heat. Add 1 cup onions, ginger, and garlic; stir fry 30 seconds. Add remaining eggs and rice; stir fry 3 minutes. Stir in half of egg strips, remaining 3/4 cup onions, remaining 1/8 teaspoon pepper, soy sauce, and peas; cook 30 seconds, stirring well to combine. Top with remaining egg strips and cilantro.

Nutritional information per serving:

Calories: 310.9, Protein: 11.4 g, Carbohydrate: 45.7 g, Dietary Fiber: 4.5 g, Total Fat: 9.4 g, Saturated Fat: 1.7 g, Cholesterol: 141 mg, Phosphorus: 278.9 mg, Potassium: 325.6 mg, Sodium: 454.2 mg

GARDEN COLESLAW WITH ALMONDS

Serves: 6   Portion Size: ¾ cup

Ingredients:

¼ cup	Roasted Almonds
1 each	Cabbage Head
1 cup	Grated Carrots
2 Tbsp	Olive Oil
3 Tbsp	Rice Vinegar
2 Tbsp	Honey
¼ cup	Greek Yogurt
1 ½ tsp	Dijon Mustard
¼ tsp	Black Pepper

Instructions:

Start by toasting the almonds; put them in a small skillet, without oil, over medium heat and shake until almonds start to get golden brown. Remove and set aside.

Make slaw by shredding cabbage and dicing. Put in bowl. Shred carrots, add to bowl.

Make dressing by whisking together the remaining ingredients until smooth; then pour the dressing over the slaw.

Add the toasted almonds, tossing to combine.

Let stand for 30 minutes, tossing several times.

To serve, spoon portions onto individual salad plates.

Nutritional information per serving:

Calories: 162.8, Protein: 5.1 g, Carbohydrate: 21.2 g, Dietary Fiber: 6.4 g, Total Fat: 7.8 g, Saturated Fat: .9 g, Cholesterol: 0 mg, Phosphorus: 103.5 mg, Potassium: 479.2 mg, Sodium: 69.3 mg

GREEN BEAN SALAD WITH QUINOA

Serves: 6   Portion Size: 1/6 of Recipe

Ingredients:

¼ cup	Olive Oil
3 Tbsp	Balsamic Vinegar
1 Tbsp	Honey
1 tsp	Minced Garlic
1 tsp	Ground Basil
½ tsp	Black Pepper
½ cup	Quinoa
2 each	Green Onions
¼ cup	Chopped Hazelnuts
¾ lb	Frozen French Cut Beans
1 cup	Water

Instructions:

Blend together olive oil, vinegar, honey, garlic, basil, and pepper to make dressing.

To make the salad, bring 1 cup water to a boil and add quinoa. Reduce heat, cover and simmer, for about 20 minutes until all liquid is absorbed. Transfer to a large mixing bowl to cool. Steam or blanch green beans until just barely soft. Drain well and add green beans to cooled quinoa. Slice green onions thinly and add with half of the chopped hazelnuts. Toss with desired amount dressing and season with fresh ground black pepper along with the rest of the hazelnuts.

Nutritional information per serving:

Calories: 198.7, Protein: 3.7 g, Carbohydrate: 18.5 g, Dietary Fiber: 3.4 g, Total Fat: 12.9 g, Saturated Fat: 1.585 g, Cholesterol: 0 mg, Phosphorus: 100.8 mg, Potassium: 239.1 mg Sodium: 161 mg

ITALIAN GREEN BEANS

Serves: 6   Portion Size: ½ cup

Ingredients:

16 ounces   Frozen Italian Beans
1 Tbsp   Olive Oil
1 cup   Chopped Onions
2 tsp   Minced Garlic
1 cup   Low Sodium Canned Diced Tomato
¼ tsp   Ground Basil
¼ tsp   Ground Oregano

Instructions:

Steam green beans until tender crisp. Set aside. Heat olive oil in a medium nonstick skillet over medium-high heat. Sauté onions until clear. Add garlic; sauté 30 seconds. Add tomatoes, basil, and oregano, and simmer for 15 to 20 minutes. Pour tomato mixture over steamed green beans and mix well.

Nutritional information per serving:

Calories: 67.1, Protein: 2.1 g, Carbohydrate: 10.9 g, Dietary Fiber: 3.6 g, Total Fat: 2.5 g, Saturated Fat: .3g, Cholesterol: 0 mg, Calcium: 66.8 mg, Phosphorus: 46.7 mg, Potassium: 215.5 mg, Sodium: 217.2 mg

ORZO WITH HERBS

Serves: 4   Portion Size: ½ cup

Ingredients:

1 cup   Cooked Orzo
2 Tbsp   Fresh Chopped Basil
¼ cup   Parsley
1 Tbsp   Olive Oil
¼ tsp   Black Pepper

Instructions:

Cook 1 cup orzo pasta according to package directions, omitting salt and fat. Drain; toss orzo with ¼ cup chopped fresh basil, 2 tablespoons chopped fresh parsley, 1 tablespoon extra-virgin olive oil, and ¼ teaspoon freshly ground black pepper.

Nutritional information per serving:

Calories: 171.2, Protein: 5.3 g, Carbohydrate: 27.6 g, Dietary Fiber: 1.8 g, Total Fat: 4.2 g, Saturated Fat: .6 g, Cholesterol: 0 mg, Phosphorus: 54.6 mg, Potassium: 65.4 mg, Sodium: 208.2 mg

ROASTED GARLIC CARROTS

Serves: 6   Portion Size: 1/6 of Recipe

Ingredients:

1 ¼ lb   Carrots
1 Tbsp   Minced Garlic
2 Tbsp   Olive Oil

Instructions:

Combine carrots, garlic, and oil; place in the baking dish. Bake at 375°F for 40 minutes or until done.

Nutritional information per serving:

Calories: 74.9, Protein: .8 g, Carbohydrate: 8.2 g, Dietary Fiber: 2.9 g, Total Fat: 4.677 g, Saturated Fat: .6 g,Cholesterol: 0 mg, Phosphorus: 30.5 mg, Potassium: 227.7 mg, Sodium: 55.1 mg

ROASTED PARMESAN ZUCCHINI

Serves: 5   Portion Size: ½ cup

Ingredients:

2 cups   Chopped Zucchini
2 tsp   Olive Oil
1 tsp   Minced Garlic
3 Tbsp   Grated Reduced Fat Parmesan Cheese

Instructions:

Preheat oven to 450°. Coat a roasting pan with cooking spray. Slice zucchini into 2 inch wedges and place in pan. Drizzle olive oil over zucchini, and sprinkle evenly with garlic and parmesan cheese. Roast for approximately 20 minutes.

Nutritional information per serving:

Calories: 33.1, Protein: 1.2 g, Carbohydrate: 1.8 g, Dietary Fiber: .5 g, Total Fat: 2.6 g, Saturated Fat: .7 g, Cholesterol: 2.6 mg, Phosphorus: 41.6 mg, Potassium: 135.5 mg, Sodium: 50 mg

SAGE SWEET POTATO TURNIP MASH

Serves: 6   *Portion Size:*   *3 ounces*

Ingredients:

½ lb	Peeled and Diced Sweet Potato
½ lb	Diced Turnip
2 tsp	Minced Garlic
1 1/3 Tbsp	Ground Sage
3 Tbsp	Unsalted Butter
½ tsp	Kosher Salt
½ tsp	Black Pepper

Instructions:

In a large saucepan, put sweet potatoes, turnips, garlic, and 1 tablespoon sage, pour in enough cold water to cover and bring pot to a boil.

Reduce heat to a medium-low and simmer until fork tender, about 10 to 15 minutes depending on the size of the vegetables.

Drain well, and keep in saucepan, covered, to keep warm.

Make Sage butter: put butter in a skillet over medium heat and when it's melted, add the 1 teaspoon sage, stirring and cooking for 1 minute, but don't let the butter burn.

Uncover the pot of vegetables and pour the sage butter over the vegetables, add the salt and black pepper, and mash with the potato masher until light and fluffy.

Nutritional information per serving:

Calories: 145.6, Protein: 1.8 g, Carbohydrate: 21.8 g, Dietary Fiber: 4.4 g, Total Fat: 6 g, Saturated Fat: 3.7 g, Cholesterol: 15.3 mg, Phosphorus: 33.3 mg, Potassium: 198.8 mg, Sodium: 173.7 mg

SAVORY GRITS

Serves: 7   Portion Size: ½ cup

Ingredients:

3 ½ cups	Water
¾ cup	Dry Grits
½ tsp	Salt
¼ cup	Chopped Onions
¼ cup	Shredded Reduced Fat Cheddar Cheese

Instructions:

In a medium saucepan, bring water to a boil. Stir in grits and salt, stirring vigorously. Reduce heat and simmer, covered, for 15 to 20 minutes, stirring occasionally. Stir in cheese and onions until cheese melts.

Nutritional information per serving:

Calories: 74.6, Protein: 2.7 g, Carbohydrate: 14.5 g, Dietary Fiber: .9 g, Total Fat: 1 g, Saturated Fat: .5 g, Cholesterol: 2.3 mg, Phosphorus: 54.4 mg, Potassium: 39 mg, Sodium: 199.5 mg

VEGETABLE PAELLA

Serves: 6   Portion Size: 1 cup

Ingredients:

1 Tbsp	Olive Oil
1 cup	Chopped Red Pepper
1 cup	Chopped Onions
1 Tbsp	Minced Garlic
1 ounce	White Wine
1 ½ cups	Uncooked White Rice
3 cups	Low Sodium Chicken Stock, (pg. 95)
2 cups	Diced Canned Tomatoes
1½ tsp	Paprika
¼ tsp	Black Pepper
15 ounces	Rinsed and Drained Canellini Beans
½ cup	Frozen Sweet Corn

Instructions:

Add oil to a large nonstick skillet over medium to high heat. Sauté bell pepper and onion for 3 to 4 minutes. Add garlic and sauté for about 30 seconds. Add wine and cook until liquid is reduced by half, about 3 minutes. Stir in rice, chicken stock, tomatoes, paprika, and pepper. Bring to a boil. Reduce heat and simmer for 25 minutes. Stir in beans and corn, and simmer for 2 more minutes until heated thoroughly.

Nutritional information per serving:

Calories: 312, Protein: 10.3 g, Carbohydrate: 58.8 g, Dietary Fiber: 5.3 g, Total Fat: 4 g, Saturated Fat: .7 g, Cholesterol: 0 mg, Phosphorus: 182 mg, Potassium: 567.9 mg, Sodium: 359.3 mg

DESSERTS

Orange and Red Loaf

Apple Blueberry Crumble

Cherries in the Snow

Fruity Cinnamon Quinoa Pudding

ORANGE AND RED LOAF

ORANGE AND RED LOAF

Serves: 20   *Portion Size:*   *1 Slice, ¾" Thick*

Ingredients:

2 ½ cups	All Purpose Flour
2 tsp	Pumpkin Pie Spice
2 tsp	Baking Powder
2 each	Whole Eggs
2 cups	Sugar
15 oz can	Pumpkin Puree
½ cup	Vegetable Oil
1 cup	Fresh or Frozen Cranberries

Instructions:

Preheat oven to 350'F. Combine flour, pumpkin pie spice, and baking powder in a large bowl. Then combine eggs, sugar, pumpkin puree and oil in another small mixing bowl. Beat until blended.

Add pumpkin puree mixture to flour mixture. Stir until just moistened, then add in cranberries and stir until cranberries are gently incorporated.

Spoon batter into 2 greased 9 x 5 inch loaf pans. Bake for 55 to 60 minutes.

Cool in pans for 5 to 10 minutes. Remove to wire rack to cool before slicing. Each pan makes 10 servings.

Nutritional information per serving:

Calories: 187, Protein 2 gm, Carbohydrate 31 gm, Fiber 1.1 gm, Fat 6 gm, Cholesterol 21 mg, Phosphorus 75 mg, Potassium 69 mg, Sodium 45 mg

APPLE BLUEBERRY CRUMBLE

Serves: 6   Portion Size: 1/6 of Recipe

Ingredients:

3 each	Medium Apples
¼ cup	Frozen Unsweetened Blueberries
¾ cup	Old Fashioned Oatmeal, Dry
1 Tbsp	Almonds
2 tsp	Packed Brown Sugar
1 Tbsp	Unsalted Butter
1 each	Egg White

Instructions:

Cut your whole apples in half, crosswise. Using a teaspoon, scoop out the seeds and hard centers. Fill the center cavity with blueberries.

In a bowl, combine oats, almonds, butter, and sugar. Whisk egg whites until frothy. Stir egg white into oats mix. Pile oats mix evenly over the fruit. Bake at 350°F for 40 minutes, until golden and apple is tender.

Nutritional information per serving:

Calories: 128.5, Protein: 2.7 g, Carbohydrate: 22.2 g, Dietary Fiber: 3.6 g, Total Fat: 4 g, Saturated Fat: 1.5 g, Cholesterol: 5.1 mg, Phosphorus: 65.2 mg, Potassium: 166.7 mg, Sodium: 11.4 mg

CHERRIES IN THE SNOW

Serves: 12   *Portion Size:*   *1/12 of Recipe*

Ingredients:

1 can	Cherry Pie Filling
1 cup	Green Grapes
2 ounces	Dry Roasted Pecans
2 cups	Miniature Marshmallows
2 cups	Lite Cool Whip

Instructions:

Place cherry pie filling in a mixing bowl. Mix in green grapes. Add pecans and marshmallows. Fold in whip topping, being sure to mix well so all ingredients are incorporated together. Cover and refrigerate until ready to serve.

Nutritional information per serving:

Calories: 150.2, Protein: 1.2 g, Carbohydrate: 25.6 g, Dietary Fiber: .8 g, Total Fat: 5.2 g, Saturated Fat: 1.7 g, Cholesterol: .25 mg Phosphorus: 32 mg Potassium: 99.8 mg, Sodium: 24.8 mg

FRUITY CINNAMON QUINOA PUDDING

Serves: 6   Portion Size: 1/6 of Recipe

Ingredients:

1 cup	Quinoa, Dry
2 cups	Water
½ cup	Craisins
¼ cup	Dried Cherries
½ cup	Apple Juice
1 tsp	Vanilla
½ tsp	Ground Cinnamon
½ cup	Frozen Unsweetened Strawberries, Thawed

Instructions:

Rinse quinoa thoroughly in cold water and add to boiling water. Reduce heat to low, cover, and simmer slowly for 7 minutes.

Add dried fruit and continue simmering, covered, for about 5 to 7 additional minutes, until all liquid is absorbed. Combine remaining ingredients in food processor, or blender, and purée until smooth while quinoa is cooking. Remove quinoa from heat and combine with puréed mixture, mixing well. Pudding can be refrigerated until ready to serve, up to 24 hours.

Nutritional information per serving:

Calories: 169.9, Protein: 4.2 g, Carbohydrate: 34.6 g, Dietary Fiber: 3.3 g, Total Fat: 1.9 g, Saturated Fat: .2 g, Cholesterol: 0 mg, Phosphorus: 135.5 mg, Potassium: 253.5 mg Sodium: 5.468 mg

INDEX

ABOUT THE AUTHOR

Thank you so much for your support and purchase of this book! I hope you will give it an honest review, that helps others decide if it's the right book for them.

I want to remind you about the free E-course that is part of this book – added information about related topics that you can use to improve your cooking and health.

Go to: http://www.renaldiethq.com/e-course-kidney-friendly-diet-cookbook/

A little bit about me, I am a registered dietitian nutritionist in Oklahoma. I have been working in the field since 1996. I have an MBA and I love to cook. I am married and have 2 children. I work as an adjunct professor locally at one of the colleges, teaching food service management. I understand making menus and how to create recipes that are healthy and tasty. As a dietitian for so long, I have spoken with many of you who struggle with chronic kidney disease, and I want to help. You can always find more information and articles at my website dedicated to that topic at: http://www.renaldiethq.com/

I also have a podcast on iTunes at: http://www.renaldiethq.com/go/itunes

I have a YouTube channel where I often do live events talking about renal and kidney disease: http://www.youtube.com/RenalDietHQ

I would love to have you in the Face book group: http://www.renaldiethq.com/facebookgroup

I also have a Google+ group if you prefer: http://www.renaldiethq.com/talkingkidneydisease

OTHER TITLES BY MATHEA FORD

Mathea Ford, Author Page (all books):

http://www.amazon.com/Mathea-Ford/e/B008E1E7IS/

The Kidney Friendly Diet Cookbook

http://www.amazon.com/Kidney-Friendly-Diet-Cookbook-PreDialysis-ebook/dp/B00BC7BGPI/

Create Your Own Kidney Diet Plan

http://www.amazon.com/Create-Your-Kidney-Diet-Plan-ebook/dp/B009PSN3R0/

Living with Chronic Kidney Disease - Pre-Dialysis

http://www.amazon.com/Living-Chronic-Kidney-Disease-Pre-Dialysis-ebook/dp/B008D8RSAQ/

Eating a Pre-Dialysis Kidney Diet - Calories, Carbohydrates, Fat & Protein, Secrets To Avoid Dialysis

http://www.amazon.com/Eating-Pre-Dialysis-Kidney-Diet-Carbohydrates-ebook/dp/B00DU2JCHM/

Eating a Pre-Dialysis Kidney Diet - Sodium, Potassium, Phosphorus and Fluids, A Kidney Disease Solution

http://www.amazon.com/Eating-Pre-Dialysis-Kidney-Diet-Phosphorus-ebook/dp/B00E2U8VMS/

Eating Out On a Kidney Diet: Pre-dialysis and Diabetes: Ways To Enjoy Your Favorite Foods

http://www.amazon.com/Eating-Out-Kidney-Diet-Pre-dialysis/dp/0615928781/

Kidney Disease: Common Labs and Medical Terminology: The Patient's Perspective

http://www.amazon.com/Kidney-Disease-Terminology-Perspective-Pre-Dialysis/dp/0615931804/

Dialysis: Treatment Options for the Progression to End Stage Renal Disease

http://www.amazon.com/Dialysis-Treatment-Options-Progression-Disease/dp/0615932258/

Mindful Eating For A Pre-Dialysis Kidney Diet: Healthy Attitudes Toward Food and Life

http://www.amazon.com/Mindful-Eating-Pre-Dialysis-Kidney-Diet/dp/0615933475/

The Emotional Challenges Of Coping with Chronic Kidney Disease

http://www.amazon.com/Emotional-Challenges-Chronic-Disease-Dialysis-ebook/dp/B00H6SYQG8/

Heart Healthy Living with Kidney Disease: Lowering Blood Pressure

http://www.amazon.com/Heart-Healthy-Living-Kidney-Disease/dp/0615936059/

Exercising with Chronic Kidney Disease: Solutions To An Active Lifestyle http://www.amazon.com/Exercising-Chronic-Kidney-Disease-Solutions/dp/0615936342/

Sexuality and Chronic Kidney Disease For Men and Women: A Path To Better Understanding

http://www.amazon.com/Sexuality-Chronic-Kidney-Disease-Women/dp/0615960197/

Anemia and Chronic Kidney Disease: Signs, Symptoms, and Treatment for Anemia in Kidney Failure

http://www.amazon.com/Anemia-Chronic-Kidney-Disease-Treatment/dp/0692201416/

Alternative Treatment Options For Chronic Kidney Failure: Natural Remedies for Living a Healthier Life

http://www.amazon.com/Alternative-Treatment-Options-Chronic-Failure/dp/0692281916/

Caring for Renal Patients: A guide to taking care of your loved ones who are struggling with kidney failure

http://www.amazon.com/Headquarters-Disease-Patients-Educational-Worksheets/dp/B00LZ2ICPW/

Positive Beginnings: The Dialysis Breakfast Cookbook

http://www.amazon.com/Positive-Beginnings-Dialysis-Breakfast-Cookbook/dp/069227958X/

Sign up for our email list to learn of new titles right away!

http://www.renaldiethq.com/go/email/

DISCLAIMER

Why I wrote this book - In my first book, I wrote extensively about how to take your pre-dialysis kidney disease and slow it down. In my second book, I wrote about how to create your own kidney diet plan and using the spreadsheets I provided – to find a way to make the process easier to do it yourself.

What I have found through the emails and requests of my readers is that it is difficult to find information about a pre-dialysis kidney diet that is actionable. I want you to know that is what I intend to provide in all my books. Especially this one. You can take these recipes and create several weeks of meals that you and your family will enjoy and they all fit a stage 2 – 5 kidney disease patient.

I wrote this book with you in mind: the person with kidney problems who does not know where to start or can't seem to get the answers that you need from other sources. This book will provide recipes that are applicable to a predialysis kidney disease diet.

Who am I? I am a registered dietitian in the USA who has been working with kidney patients for my entire 15 + years of experience. I have a website that provides renal diet meal plans for all stages of kidney disease – check it out at http://www.renaldiethq.com/predialysis-cookbook/. Find all my books on amazon on my author page: http://www.amazon.com/Mathea-Ford/e/B008E1E7IS/

My goals are simple – to give some answers and to create an understanding of what is typical. It will not necessarily be what happens in your case, as everyone is an individual. I may simplify things in an effort to write them so that I feel you can learn the most from the information. This may mean that I don't say the exact things that your doctor would say. If you don't understand, please ask your doctor.

I want you to know, I am not a medical doctor and I am not aware of your particular condition. Information in this book is current as of publication, but may or may not have changed. This book is not meant to substitute for medical treatment for you, your friends, your caregivers, or your family members. You should not base treatment decisions solely on what is contained in this book. Develop your treatment plan with your doctors, nurses and the other medical professionals on your team. I recommend that you double-check any information with your medical team to verify if it applies to you.

In other words, I am not responsible for your medical care. I am providing this book for information and entertainment purposes, not medical diagnoses. Please consult with your doctor about any questions that you have about your particular case.

Made in the USA
Las Vegas, NV
21 June 2022

50532821R00083